CLEAN EATING

Copyright 2018 © Tamarind Press

No part of this publication may be reproduced, stored in a retrieval system or transmitted in any form or by any means, electronic, mechanical, photocopying, recording, scanning or otherwise, without the prior written permission of the Publisher.

The Publisher and the authors make no representations or warranties with respect to the accuracy or completeness of the contents of this work and specifically disclaim all warranties, including without limitation warranties of fitness for a particular purpose. The advice and strategies contained herein may not be suitable for every situation. This work is sold with the understanding that the publisher is not engaged in redering medical, legal or other professional advice or services. Neither the publisher nor the authors shall be liable for damages arising herefrom. The fact that an individual, organization or website is referred to in this work as a citation and/or potential source of further information does not mean that the authors or the Publisher endorses the information the individual, organization or website may provide or recommendations it/they may make. Further, readers should be aware that Internet websites listed in this work may have changed or disappeared between when this work was written and when it is read.

Tamarind Press publishers its books in a variety of electronic and print formats. Some content that appears in print may not be available in electronic books, and vice versa.

Trademarks: Tamarind Press and Tamarind Press logo are trademarks or registered trademarks of Happy Self Publishing, and may not be used without written permission. All other trademarks are the property of the respective owners. Tamarind Press is not associated with any product or vendor mentioned in this book.

Photo credits: 123rf.com

First Edition 2018

ASIN: B07BRSZ48N

ISBN: 9781980678144

Published by Tamarind Press
Website: www.tamarindpress.com

Claim Your Free Bonus

Weekly meal plan & Grocery Shopping List

Our goal is not just to inspire you with healthy recipes but also encourage you to try them inside your kitchen as a step towards adopting a healthier lifestyle. Therefore, to make things super easy for you, our team has created a 7-day meal plan and a grocery shopping list to accompany it.

Go to www.tamarindpress.com/clean-eating-bonus to download the handy PDF.

If you enjoyed reading the book, don't forget to leave a quick review inside Amazon. As a token of thanks, we'll send you the ebook version of our next cookbook (absolutely for FREE!). Just drop us an email to review@tamarindpress.com after you review the book to claim another awesome cookbook!

Contents

Introduction 6
What is Clean Eating 6
Benefits of Clean Eating 8
How to adapt Clean Eating principles to your busy daily life 9
Grocery Shopping Suggestions 10
What to choose: 11
What to avoid: 11

Salads 14
Fresh Tuna and Spinach Salad 15
Tropical Salad 16
Lemon-Basil Chicken Salad 17
Mediterranean Salad 18
Cabbage and Apple Salad 19
Avocado and Chickpea Salad 20
Orange and Walnut Salad 21
Healthy Caesar's Salad 22
Turmeric Chicken Salad 23
Raw Salmon Salad 24
Artichokes, Tofu and Quinoa Salad 26
Quinoa and Chicory Salad 27
Beet and Spinach Salad 28
Colorful Salad 29
Egg and Avocado Salad 30
Endive and Chicory Salad 31
Asparagus and Parmesan Salad 32
Chicken and Avocado Salad 33
Barley and Walnut Salad 34
Pear Salad 36
Grapefruit and Avocado Salad 37
Bean and Kale Salad 38
Fresh Tuna Salad 39
Summer Quinoa Salad 40
Fennel and Shrimp Salad 41
Grape and Kale Salad 42
Barley and Crab Salad 43
Brussels Salad 44
Shrimps and Beans Salad 45
Mango and Scallops Salad 46
Fresh Tuna and Egg Salad 48
Chicken and Melon Salad 49
Edamame Salad 50
Barley and Pumpkin Salad 51
Quinoa with Beets and Walnuts 52

Main Courses 54
Grilled Lemon Chicken 55
Chicken and Asparagus Rolls 56
Grilled Lamb 57
Garlic Brown Rice with Black Beans 58
Eggplant Lasagna 59
Turmeric Brown Rice with Edamame 60
Sesame Salmon 62
Curry Salmon 63
Grilled Lamb with Apple Sauce 64
Lamb Meatballs 65
Green Tea Halibut 66
Spicy Prawns 67

Eggs with Beans and Avocado   68
Stir-Fried Veggies   70
Instant Pot Garlic Chicken   71
Chickpea Burger   72
Broccoli Burger   73
Veggie Balls   74
Fish Balls   75
Grilled Chicken with Peppers   76
Pumpkin and Chicken Curry   78
Eggplant Burger   79
Walnut Burger   80
Brown Rice with Beans   81
Cauliflower and Chickpea Curry   82
Brown Rice with Beets   83
Quinoa with Eggplants   84
Spicy Edamame with Shrimps   86
Cous Cous with Stir-Fried Veggies   87
Salmon Fillet with Ginger Apple Sauce   88
Orange Chicken   89
Basil Grilled Vegetables   90
Steamed Chicken with Brussels   91
Barley with Mushrooms   92
Eggs and Veggies   93
Veggie Skewers   94
Hazelnut Chicken   95
Lamb with Red Onion Sauce   96
Grilled Bass with Spring Onions   97
Spicy Cauliflower   98
Chicken Chili   99
Mediterranean Chicken   100
Lime Salmon   101

Snacks/Appetizers   102
Sweet Potato Waffles   103
Pepper Omelet   104
Vegetarian Wraps   105
Buckwheat Pancakes with Broccoli and Leek   106
Zucchini Pancakes with Leek and Avocado   107
Scrambled Eggs with Mushrooms   108
Turmeric Quinoa Balls   109
Lentil Falafel   110
Savory Oatmeal   112
Hummus with veggies   113
Sweet Potato Muffins   114
Cottage Cheese Savory Pancakes   115
Salmon Rolls with Avocado Sauce   116

Soups   118
Leek and Potato Soup   119
Shrimp Soup   120
Carrot and Coconut Soup   121
Spinach and Broccoli Soup   122
Ginger Bean Cream   124
Tomato Soup   125
Cauliflower Soup   126
Carrot and Ginger Soup   127
Mushroom Soup   128

Conversion Chart   130

Introduction

What is Clean Eating

Nowadays, there is a lot of talk about "Clean Eating", which is a food philosophy promoted by Tosca Reno (an American nutritionist author of the "Eat-Clean Diet" series), so let's discover in detail what it is all about, exactly.

This food theory basically promotes the concept of eating in as natural a way as possible, which means choosing fresh foods, which are not packaged nor processed in any way, in the exact shape nature made them.

What should be banned in this kind of nutrition?

- **Refined foods:** this definition refers to a manufacturing process involving foods rich in carbs, like grains and sugars, which are whitened to obtain a more appealing texture and a longer shelf life (ex: white flour, white rice etc.). In alternative, whole grains should be preferred (ex: brown rice, quinoa etc.);

- **Processed foods:** almost every packaged food has been processed in some ways. The main categories include:

  - Frozen foods (ex: ready meals)

  - Canned foods (ex: canned peaches or fruit juices)

  - Processed foods often contain chemical substances which are potentially damaging for the consumers' health and they lose most of their nutrients during the manufacturing process;

- **Additives:** most of the packaged foods in supermarkets contain at least a couple of them. They can be:

  - Artificial food colors: they are used to make food look more appealing (ex: candies, cheese, jams etc.)

  - Preservatives: they are used to extend a product's shelf life to match the needs of large supermarket chains

  - Vitamins and salts: they seem to be a great addiction to make food items healthier, but they are chemical substances which alter the original composition. Foods with "less" of something (ex: less sodium canned soups) should be avoided too;

  - Added salt, sugar or fat: they are usually added to improve flavors and aromas, but they also stimulate the production of dopamine, a neurotransmitter associated with pleasure, which gives addiction and drives people to eat more than necessary;

At its purest, Clean Eating consists of only choosing raw ingredients, so fully unprocessed, but cooking can also improve the organoleptic characteristics of certain foods, so that it's best to alternate raw and cooked meals. Of course, cooking with animal fats and frying should be avoided, but you don't necessarily have to change your nutritional style completely, nor your settled habits. In most cases, quick cooking methods, like griddling, stir-frying or steaming, give you the chance to eat exactly the same food you are used to, by preserving all their nutrients.

Basically, Clean Eating is similar to a plant-based diet, but you can also include eggs, meat and fish in your daily meals, provided they are fresh and free of chemical additives.

What to check, then?

- Eggs: they shall be fresh and possibly organic;

- Meat: it shall be lean, boneless, skinless and coming from grass-fed animals. You should also make sure that animals have not been given antibiotics or other artificial substances to speed-up their growth;

- Fish: it shall come from sustainable fishing and be free of mercury;

Clean Eating philosophy suggests to have 5-6 meals a day, to avoid drops in physical energy and maintain metabolism. It's easier than you may think, and you just have to divide your meals into breakfast, morning snack, lunch, afternoon snack and dinner to comply with this rule.

The main meals (breakfast, lunch and dinner) should include carbs, proteins and fat and you shall have at least 5 servings of fruits and vegetables each day (ex: fruits for breakfast and snacks and vegetables for lunch and dinner).

You should also pay attention to what you drink: fruit juices should be avoided, since they're full of added sugar, as much as coffee and alcohol, of course. In alternative, you can buy fresh oranges to squeeze, have green tea (with some mint or honey to be added for some extra flavor) and a lot of water.

Last but not least, a Clean Eating lifestyle also include regular exercise, the right amount of sleep and respect for the environment.

Benefits of Clean Eating

- It has been scientifically demonstrated that Clean Eating principles (eating plenty of fruits and vegetables, less sugar, less salt and no processed foods) help prevent several diseases, especially diabetes and cardiovascular problems, while taking care of intestinal flora and brain health;

- Following these nutritional requirements, you can also avoid obesity and stay fit with zero effort;

- Your daily amount of greens will help your skin and hair look healthy, young and strong;

- Last but not least, Clean Eating is also environmentally friendly and it helps the preservation of natural resources: buying fresh and local food reduces the pollution caused by transportation and avoiding packages reduces the amount of plastic and waste. Moreover, buying local food also helps the economy of small communities;

How to adapt Clean Eating principles to your busy daily life

If you are used to a busy life with long working hours, you'll probably pay little attention to what you eat and you just grab the first ready meal available in the frozen food department of the closet supermarket. In this case, a Clean Eating diet could seem difficult, tricky and time consuming, but it's not always the case, if you learn to be organized and adopt a few smart strategies:

- Start planning your meals on a weekly basis: if you just save 15 minutes of your Friday night to think about your meals for the next 7 days, you'll save tons of time during your busy week. You just need to figure out breakfast, snack, lunch and dinner options to avoid thinking about what to eat every single day. Moreover, setting aside a few minutes to specifically think about nutrition and meals, you have more chance to set-up healthy menus and choose the right ingredients for fresh and simple recipes.

- Set-up a complete and detailed grocery list to be able to buy your ingredients in one go: this way, you can store all the heathy food items you need and you won't yield to the temptation of eating junk food out of stress and lack of time. You just need to plan a short mid-week trip to the greengrocer to save time and money too: having a detailed grocery list allows you to just buy the exact quantities of each ingredient that you'll need during the following days, avoiding any kind of waste.

- Be inspired by the recipes you'll find in this book, to prepare delicious meals ready in less than 30 minutes!

Grocery Shopping Suggestions

The best way to make sure you buy fresh and healthy ingredients is going shopping at the closest farmers' market, instead of preferring large supermarket chains: this way, you can talk directly to the vendors and ask them about the origin of meat, fish and greens. Moreover, it is easier to find unpackaged and unprocessed foods, which will naturally push you towards healthier choices and will also let you save some money, since plastic bags and cellophane are expensive.

If you cannot avoid supermarkets and a small amount of packaged foods, the best thing you can do is carefully reading labels: they shall not list too many ingredients and the main ones (ex: milk for yogurt or wheat for bread) should be at the top. If you read the name of some chemical substances, or you see secondary ingredients at the top of the label (ex: sugar in yogurt or salt in bread), you should search for an alternative product. On the other hand, supermarkets can offer the opportunity to have discounts on buying great quantities of certain foods: for example, you can buy big packages of dried beans or whole grains, which can be stored for longer periods and you can use in several different ways.

If you are not used to paying attention to what you eat, you can start with small steps, not to feel overwhelmed and demotivated. For example, you can just replace one food item at a time with its healthier substitute, as soon as you run out of it: if you have to replace your empty rice jar, choose brown rice instead of white one, or if you have to buy something for breakfast, choose oatmeal instead of packaged cereals.

What to choose:

- Fresh fruits and vegetables (preferably seasonal and organic)
- Natural oils (olive, avocado, coconut, flaxseed etc.)
- Legumes (beans, chickpeas, edamame etc.)
- Nuts and seeds (almonds, hazelnuts, walnuts etc.)
- Fresh eggs
- Organic meat and fish
- Low-fat dairy (organic milk, parmesan cheese, plain yogurt etc.)
- Whole grains (oats, quinoa, brown rice etc.)
- Whole flours (whole wheat flour, coconut flour, almond flour etc.)
- Natural sweeteners (honey, maple syrup etc.)
- Herbs and spices to season food without adding too much salt

What to avoid:

- Processed meat (sausages, cold cuts etc.)
- Canned food items
- Sauces (mayonnaise, ketchup etc.)
- Dried fruits
- Soft drinks
- Fruits and vegetables grown with the use of pesticides and chemical additives
- Pasta, white rice, white bread, biscuits etc.
- White sugar
- Butter and animal fats

CLEAN EATING

Weeknight Dinners

100 FAST & HEALTHY DINNER RECIPES
(READY IN UNDER 30 MINS)

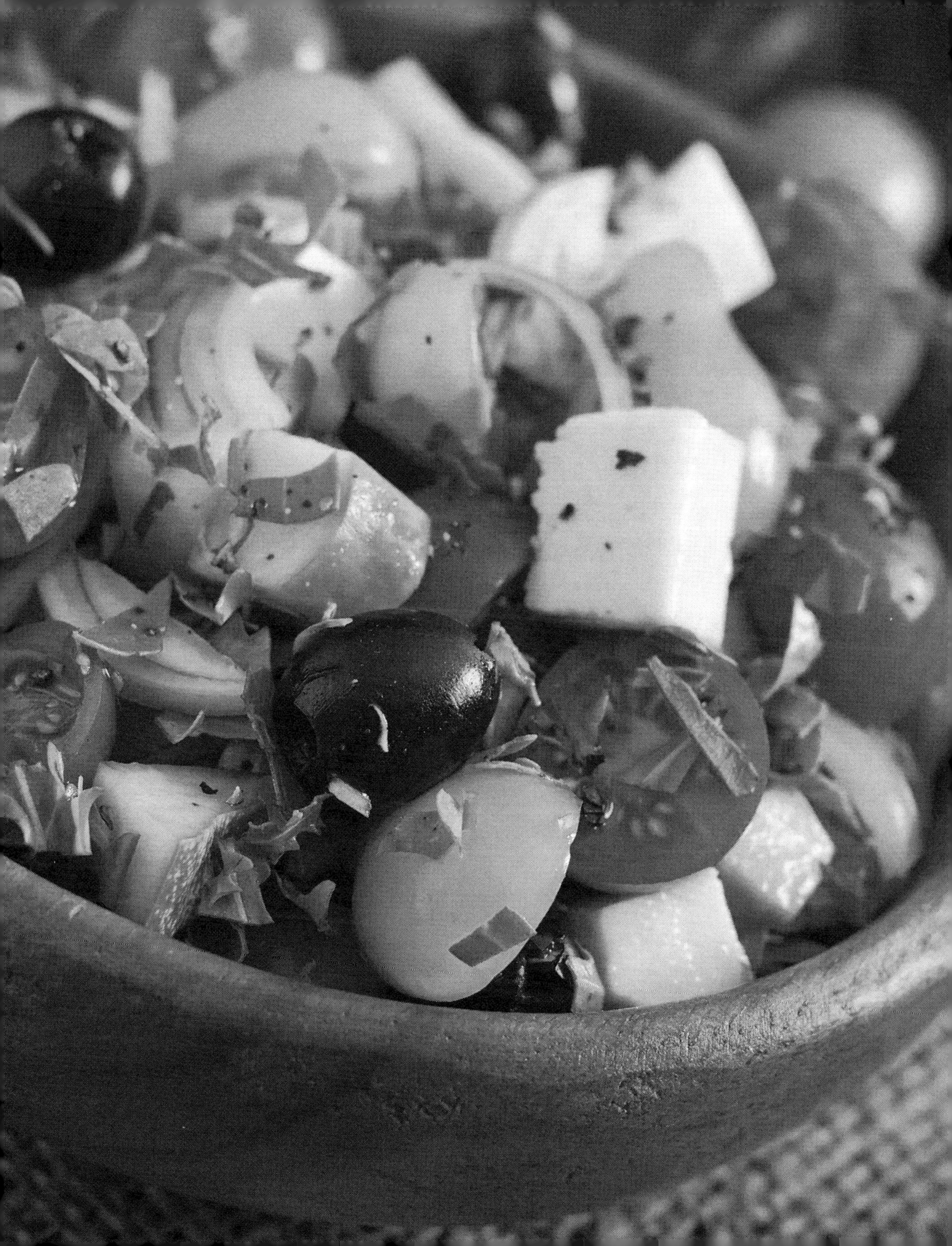

Salads

Fresh Tuna and Spinach Salad

Servings: **2** • Time: **15** minutes

Ingredients:

- 1 lb baby spinach
- 5 oz fresh tuna fillet
- 2 oranges
- 2 tbsp lemon juice
- 2 tbsp olive oil
- Fresh parsley to taste

Preparation:

- Wash and chop baby spinach leaves;
- Peel and slice oranges;
- Wash and mince fresh parsley;
- Quickly grill the fresh tuna fillet (2 minutes per side), then cut it into small cubes;
- In a bowl, mix grilled tuna, oranges, spinach and parsley;
- Season your salad with lemon juice and olive oil;

Tropical Salad

Servings: **2** • Time: **10 minutes**

Ingredients:

- 1 mango
- 1 avocado
- ½ pineapple
- ½ lime (juiced)
- 2 tbsp apple cider vinegar
- 2 tbsp olive oil
- 2 tsp cumin seeds
- 1 tsp smoked paprika
- Almonds to taste
- Sesame seeds to taste
- Fresh cilantro leaves to taste

Preparation:

- Peel and slice avocado;
- Spread some lime juice over avocado slices;
- Peel and slice mango;
- Peel and slice pineapple;
- Wash cilantro leaves;
- In a large bowl, mix mango, avocado, pineapple, almonds, sesame seeds and cilantro leaves;
- Season with cider vinegar, olive oil, smoked paprika and cumin seeds;

Lemon-Basil Chicken Salad

Servings: **2** • Time: **25** minutes

Ingredients:

- 10 oz arugula
- 7 oz boneless, skinless chicken breast
- 2 oz almonds
- 1 stalk celery
- 1 clove garlic
- 3 tbsp lemon juice
- 2 tbsp olive oil
- ½ tsp salt
- ½ tsp black pepper
- Fresh basil to taste

Preparation:

- Prepare a marinade with 1 tbsp olive oil, lemon juice, minced garlic, salt and black pepper;
- Cut your chicken breast into small cubes and place them in a sterile plastic bag together with the marinade;
- Shake the bag to let chicken chops fully absorb the condiment;
- Wash arugula and basil leaves and dry them;
- Wash and chop celery;
- In a bowl, mix arugula, celery, basil leaves and almonds;
- Grill chicken chops for 7-8 minutes per side (depending on their size), while pouring some marinade from time to time to keep them soft and juicy;
- Add chicken chops to your salad and season with one more tbsp olive oil;

Mediterranean Salad

Servings: **2** • Time: **20** minutes

Ingredients:

- 7 oz arugula
- 3 oz green beans
- 3 tomatoes
- 2 cucumbers
- 1 green pepper
- 1 red onion
- ½ lemon (juiced)
- 3 tbsp olive oil
- 1 tsp salt
- 1 tsp black pepper
- Fresh basil to taste
- Fresh oregano to taste

Preparation:

- Peel and slice onion;
- Wash and chop tomatoes and green pepper;
- Peel and chop cucumber;
- Steam green beans for 3-4 minutes and chop them;
- Wash and dry arugula, basil and oregano leaves;
- In a large bowl, mix arugula, basil leaves, cucumbers, tomatoes, green beans, green pepper and red onion;
- Season with lemon juice, olive oil, minced fresh oregano, salt and pepper;

Cabbage and Apple Salad

Servings: **2** • Time: **15 minutes**

Ingredients:

- 2 apples
- 1 stalk celery
- 1/2 head of cabbage
- ¼ cup walnuts
- 2 tbsp lemon juice
- 2 tbsp olive oil
- 1 tsp black pepper
- Fresh parsley to taste

Preparation:

- Wash and chop cabbage leaves and celery;
- Peel and chop apples;
- Pour lemon juice over chopped apples;
- Wash, dry and mince parsley;
- In a large bowl, mix cabbage, apples, celery, walnuts and parsley;
- Season with olive oil and black pepper;

Avocado and Chickpea Salad

Servings: **4** • Time: **30** minutes

Ingredients:

- 14 oz chickpeas (already soaked overnight)
- 12 cherry tomatoes
- 2 avocados
- 1 yellow pepper
- ½ onion
- 2 tbps olive oil
- 2 tbsp lemon juice
- 1 tsp salt
- 1 tsp black pepper
- Fresh parsley to taste

Preparation:

- Peel and slice avocados;
- Pour lemon juice over avocado slices;
- Steam chickpeas for 20 minutes;
- Wash cherry tomatoes and cut them in halves;
- Peel and slice onion;
- Wash and mince parsley;
- Wash and chop yellow pepper;
- Mix all the vegetables in a bowl and season with olive oil, lemon juice, salt and black pepper;

Orange and Walnut Salad

Servings: **4** • Time: **10 minutes**

Ingredients:

- 1 cup walnuts
- 3 whole oranges + 1 juiced
- 2 apples
- 1 lime (juiced)
- ½ red cabbage
- 2 tbsp olive oil
- 1 tsp salt

Preparation:

- Wash and chop red cabbage;
- Peel and slice oranges and apples;
- Mix all the ingredients in a bowl and season with orange juice, lime juice, olive oil and salt;

Healthy Caesar's Salad

Servings: **4** • Time: **30** minutes

Ingredients:

- 16 oz boneless, skinless chicken breast
- 3 oz chopped parmesan cheese
- 4 slices of whole wheat bread
- 1 head of kale
- 1 clove garlic
- 3 tbsp olive oil
- 2 tbsp pine nuts
- 2 tbsp lemon juice
- 2 tbsp apple cider vinegar
- 1 tsp salt
- 1 tsp black pepper

Preparation:

- Wash and dry kale leaves;
- Rub whole wheat bread with the garlic clove and a few drops of olive oil;
- Dice your bread and toast it in the oven for 7-8 minutes;
- In a small bowl, mix olive oil, lemon juice, apple cider vinegar and black pepper, to obtain a vinaigrette;
- Chop your chicken breast and rub it with salt, olive oil and lemon juice;
- Grill chicken chops for 7-8 minutes per side (depending on their size);
- In a bowl, place kale leaves, then add grilled chicken chops, toasted bread, pine nuts, parmesan cheese and season with the prepared vinaigrette;

Turmeric Chicken Salad

Servings: **2** • Time: **20** minutes

Ingredients:

- 10 oz boneless, skinless chicken breast
- 4 oz pecan nuts
- 1 head lettuce
- 1 onion
- 1 cucumber
- 1 yellow pepper
- 2 tbsp lemon juice
- 1 tbsp olive oil
- 1 tbsp sesame oil
- 2 tsp turmeric
- 2 tsp salt
- 1 tsp black pepper

Preparation:

- Cut your chicken breast into small stripes;
- Mix olive oil, turmeric, lemon juice, salt and pepper in a sterile plastic bag;
- Place your chicken stripes in the plastic bag and shake it to let the meat fully absorb all the flavors;
- Chop pecan nuts;
- Wash and chop lettuce;
- Peel cucumber and onion and slice them;
- Wash and chop yellow pepper;
- Place lettuce leaves in a bowl and add cucumber, onion and yellow pepper;
- Season with some salt and olive oil;
- Stir-fry chicken strips with sesame oil for about 5 minutes;
- Place your chicken stripes on top of raw vegetables;
- Sprinkle with pecan nuts;

Raw Salmon Salad

Servings: **4** • Time: **15 minutes**

Ingredients:

- 12 oz boneless salmon
- 6 oz baby spinach
- 2 cucumbers
- 1 red onion
- 1 lemon (juiced)
- 1 cm grated ginger root
- 1 tsp salt
- Fresh dill to taste

Preparation:

- Finely slice salmon;
- Wash, dry and mince fresh dill;
- In a bowl, mix lemon juice, grated ginger and salt;
- Spread the marinade over salmon slices;
- Peel and slice cucumber and red onion;
- Wash and dry baby spinach;
- In a bowl, place baby spinach, cucumber and red onion;
- Add salmon stripes;
- Sprinkle with minced dill;

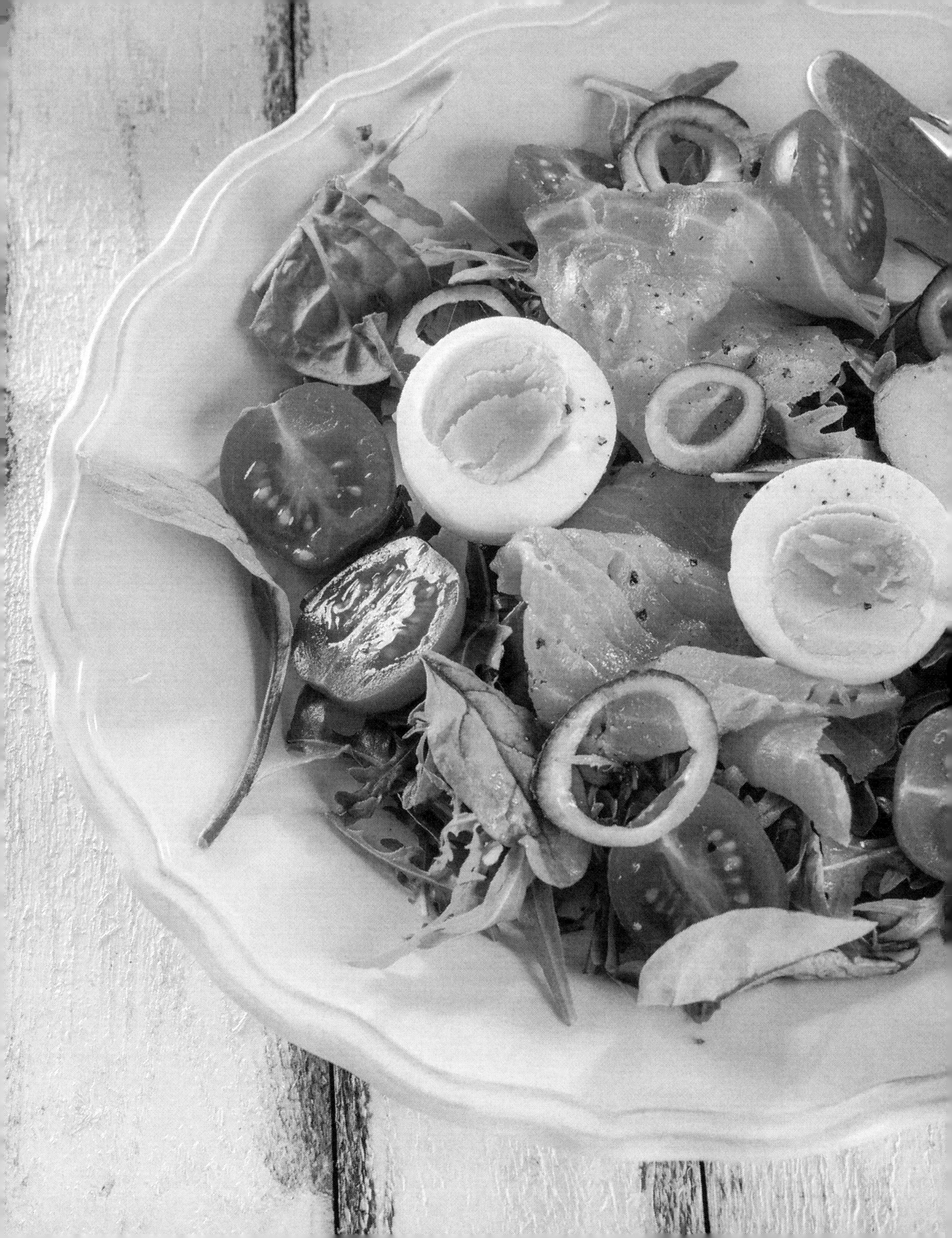

Artichokes, Tofu and Quinoa Salad

Servings: **4** • Time: **30** minutes

Ingredients:

- 1 lb artichokes
- 3 cups quinoa
- 2 cups diced tofu
- 1 lemon (juiced)
- 1 clove garlic
- 2 tbsp olive oil
- 1 tsp salt
- 1 tsp black pepper
- Fresh rosemary to taste

Preparation:

- Cook quinoa in boiling water for 20 minutes;
- Peel and finely chop garlic;
- Wash, dry and mince rosemary;
- In a small bowl, mix lemon juice, olive oil, salt, pepper, minced garlic and rosemary;
- Clean and chop the artichokes;
- Steam them for 15 minutes;
- In a bowl, mix quinoa, artichokes and tofu and season with the prepared vinaigrette;

Quinoa and Chicory Salad

Servings: **4** • Time: **20** minutes

Ingredients:

- 1 lb chicory
- 1 cup quinoa
- 1 green pepper
- 1 yellow pepper
- 1 lemon (juiced)
- 3 tbsp olive oil
- 2 tsp salt
- 1 tsp black pepper

Preparation:

- Carefully rinse quinoa and cook it in boiling water for 15 minutes;
- In the meantime, wash and dry chicory leaves and chop them;
- Wash and chop green and yellow pepper;
- In a bowl, mix quinoa, chicory, green and yellow pepper and adjust of salt and black pepper;
- Season with lemon juice and olive oil;

Beet and Spinach Salad

Servings: **4** • Time: **20 minutes**

Ingredients:

- 1 lb baby spinach
- 10 oz beets
- ½ cup walnuts
- 2 tbsp apple cider vinegar
- 2 tbsp olive oil
- 1 tbsp honey
- 1 tsp salt

Preparation:

- Wash and dry baby spinach;
- Peel and steam beets for 10 minutes;
- In a small bowl, mix olive oil, apple cider vinegar and honey to obtain a vinaigrette;
- Mix spinach, beets and walnuts and adjust with salt;
- Season with the prepared vinaigrette;

Colorful Salad

Servings: **4** • Time: **20** minutes

Ingredients:

- 14 oz lentils (already soaked overnight)
- ½ cup pomegranate seeds
- 8 radishes
- 2 cucumbers
- 1 red pepper
- 1 onion
- 1 orange (juiced)
- 2 tbsp olive oil
- 2 tsp salt
- Fresh parsley to taste

Preparation:

- Steam lentils for 20 minutes;
- Wash and slice radishes;
- Peel and slice onion on cucumber;
- Wash and chop red pepper;
- Wash, dry and mince parsley;
- Mix all the ingredients in a bowl and season with olive oil, orange juice and salt;

Egg and Avocado Salad

Servings: **2** • Time: **15 minutes**

Ingredients:

- 4 eggs
- 2 avocados
- 2 stalks celery
- 1 onion
- 1 lemon (juiced)
- 2 tbsp apple cider vinegar
- 2 tbsp olive oil
- 1 tsp salt
- 1 tsp black pepper
- 1 tsp smoked paprika

Preparation:

- Boil eggs for 10 minutes;
- Peel and slice avocados;
- Pour lemon juice over avocado slices;
- Peel and slice onion;
- Wash and chop celery;
- In a bowl, mix avocado, onion and celery and season with olive oil, apple cider vinegar, salt, black pepper and smoked paprika;
- Slice boiled eggs and place them on top of your vegetables salad;

Endive and Chicory Salad

Servings: **2** • Time: **10** minutes

Ingredients:

- ½ cup almonds
- 2 endives
- 2 oranges
- 1 fennel
- 1 chicory
- 2 tbsp apple cider vinegar
- 2 tbsp olive oil
- 1 tsp black pepper
- Fresh dill to taste;

Preparation:

- Wash and slice endives and chicory;
- Peel and slice oranges;
- Clean and slice fennel;
- Wash, dry and mince dill;
- Roast almonds;
- Place endives, chicory, fennel, oranges and almonds in a bowl and season with apple cider vinegar, olive oil and minced dill;

Asparagus and Parmesan Salad

Servings: **4** • Time: **20** minutes

Ingredients:

- 12 oz asparagus
- 7 oz parmesan cheese
- ½ cup almonds
- 2 oranges (juiced)
- 1 head of lettuce
- 2 tbsp olive oil
- 1 tsp salt
- 1 tsp black pepper

Preparation:

- Clean and steam asparagus for 10 minutes;
- Chop them;
- Wash and chop lettuce;
- Chop parmesan cheese;
- Roast almonds;
- In a small bowl, mix orange juice, olive oil, salt and black pepper to obtain a vinaigrette;
- In a bowl, mix lettuce, chopped asparagus, chopped parmesan cheese and almonds;
- Season with the prepared vinaigrette;

Chicken and Avocado Salad

Servings: **4** • Time: **20 minutes**

Ingredients:

- 1 lb boneless skinless chicken breast
- 4 tomatoes
- 3 eggs
- 2 avocados
- 2 tbsp olive oil
- 2 tbsp apple cider vinegar
- 2 tbsp lemon juice
- 2 tsp salt
- Fresh chives to taste

Preparation:

- Cut your chicken breast into small cubes and grill them for 7-8 minutes per side (according to their size);
- In the meantime, boil your eggs for 10 minutes, then peel them and cut them in halves;
- Wash, dry and mince chives;
- Peel and slice avocados;
- Pour lemon juice over avocado slices;
- Wash and chop tomatoes;
- In a bowl, mix grilled chicken, boiled eggs, avocadoes, tomatoes and chives;
- Season with olive oil, apple cider vinegar and salt;

Barley and Walnut Salad

Servings: **4** • Time: **25** minutes

Ingredients:

- 1 cup barley (already soaked overnight)
- ½ cup walnuts
- 2 peaches
- 1 red pepper
- 1 orange (juiced)
- 2 tbsp olive oil
- 2 tbsp lemon juice
- 1 tsp salt
- Fresh parsley to taste

Preparation:

- Steam barley for 20 minutes;
- Wash and cut your pepper into small stripes;
- Grill them for a couple of minutes;
- Peel and slice peaches;
- Wash, dry and mince parsley;
- In a small bowl mix orange juice, lemon juice, olive oil and salt to obtain a vinaigrette;
- In a large bowl, mix barley, walnuts, peaches, grilled pepper and parsley;
- Season your salad with the prepared vinaigrette;

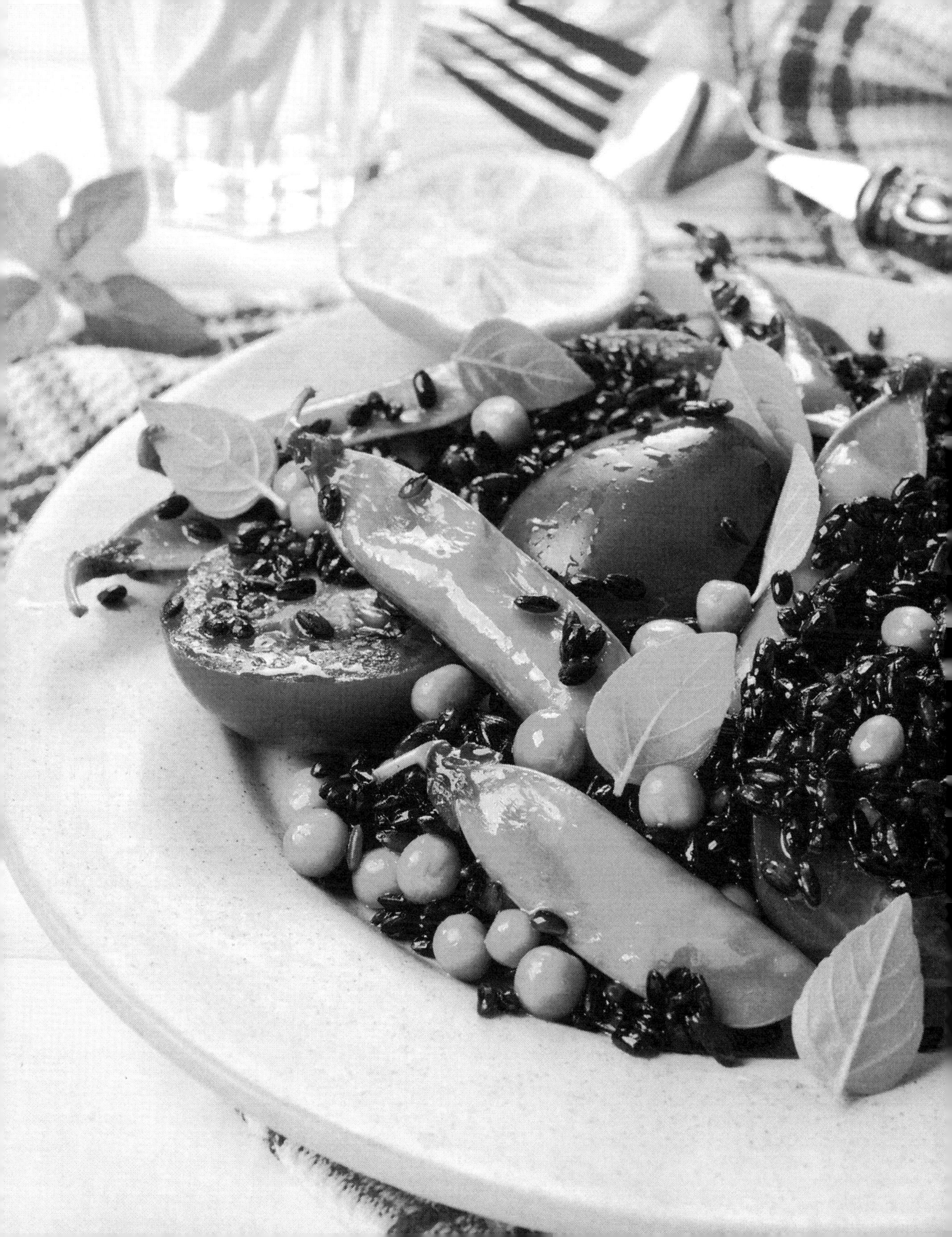

Pear Salad

Servings: **4** • Time: **30 minutes**

Ingredients:

- 2 cups mâche
- 1 cup lentils (already soaked overnight)
- 3 pears
- 2 beets
- 2 tbsp maple syrup (sugar free)
- 2 tbsp sesame oil
- 2 tbsp lemon juice
- 1 tsp salt

Preparation:

- Peel and chop beets;
- Steam lentils and beets for 20 minutes;
- Wash and dry mâche;
- Wash and chop pears;
- Pour lemon juice over pear chops;
- In a small bowl, mix sesame oil, maple syrup and salt to obtain a vinaigrette;
- In a large bowl, mix mâche, lentils, beets and pears;
- Season your salad with the prepared vinaigrette;

Grapefruit and Avocado Salad

Servings: **4** • Time: **10 minutes**

Ingredients:

- ½ cup plain yogurt
- 4 oz tofu
- 2 grapefruits
- 2 avocados
- 1 head lettuce
- 2 tbsp lemon juice
- 1 tbsp honey
- 1 tsp salt
- 1 tsp black pepper

Preparation:

- Peel and slice grapefruits;
- Peel and slice avocados;
- Pour lemon juice over avocado slices;
- Wash and chop lettuce leaves;
- Dice tofu;
- In a small bowl, mix yogurt, honey, salt and black pepper;
- In a large bowl, mix lettuce, grapefruit, avocado and tofu;
- Season your salad with the yogurt dressing;

Bean and Kale Salad

Servings: **4** • Time: **30** minutes

Ingredients:

- 1 cup beans (already soaked overnight)
- 1 cup cherry tomatoes
- 9 oz green beans
- 1 head of kale
- 1 orange (juiced)
- 2 tbsp olive oil
- 2 tsp smoked paprika

Preparation:

- Steam black beans for 20 minutes;
- Steam green beans for 10 minutes;
- Wash and chop kale leaves;
- Wash cherry tomatoes and cut them in half;
- In a small bowl, mix orange juice, olive oil and paprika to obtain a vinaigrette;
- In a large bowl, mix beans, kale, cherry tomatoes and green beans;
- Season with the prepared vinaigrette;

Fresh Tuna Salad

Servings: **4** • Time: **15 minutes**

Ingredients:

- 8 oz fresh tuna
- ¼ cup plain yogurt
- 3 tomatoes
- 1 head lettuce
- 1 onion
- 2 tbsp lemon juice
- 1 tbsp olive oil
- 1 tsp salt
- Fresh parsley to taste
- Fresh basil to taste
- Fresh chives to taste

Preparation:

- Quickly grill the fresh tuna fillet (2 minutes per side), then cut it into small cubes;
- Wash and chop tomatoes;
- Peel and slice onion;
- Wash and chop lettuce;
- Wash, dry and mince parsley, basil and chives;
- In a small bowl, mix yogurt, lemon juice, salt and olive oil;
- Mix all the ingredients in a large bowl and season with the prepared yogurt sauce;

Summer Quinoa Salad

Servings: **4** • Time: **20** minutes

Ingredients:

- 1 cup quinoa
- 16 cherry tomatoes
- 3 peaches
- 1 orange
- 1 red onion
- 1 lime (juiced)
- 2 tbsp olive oil
- Fresh thyme to taste

Preparation:

- Cook quinoa in boiling water for 10 minutes;
- Peel and chop peaches and red onion;
- Peel and slice the orange;
- Wash cherry tomatoes and cut them in half;
- Wash and dry thyme leaves;
- Mix all the ingredients in a bowl and season with lime juice and olive oil;

Fennel and Shrimp Salad

Servings: **4** • Time: **15 minutes**

Ingredients:

- 12 oz shrimps (already cleaned)
- 10 oz baby spinach
- 16 cherry tomatoes
- 2 fennels
- ½ red onion
- 2 tbsp olive oil
- 2 tbsp apple cider vinegar
- 1 tsp salt

Preparation:

- Steam shrimps for 5 minutes;
- Clean and slice fennel;
- Wash cherry tomatoes and cut them in half;
- Peel and slice red onion;
- Wash and dry baby spinach;
- Mix all the ingredients in a bowl and season with olive oil, apple cider vinegar and salt;

Grape and Kale Salad

Servings: **2** • Time: **15 minutes**

Ingredients:

- 1 cup red grape
- 6 oz kale leaves
- 4 oz salmon
- 1 shallot
- 1 apple
- 2 tbsp olive oil
- 2 tbsp apple cider vinegar
- 1 tbsp lemon juice
- 1 tsp salt
- 1 tsp black pepper

Preparation:

- Peel and slice apple;
- Pour lemon juice over apple slices;
- Peel and slice shallot;
- Wash red grapes and cut them in half;
- Wash and chop kale leaves;
- Grill salmon for a couple of minutes, then cut it into small cubes;
- In a bowl, mix shallot, apple, grape, kale leaves and grilled salmon and adjust with salt and pepper;
- Season your salad with olive oil and apple cider vinegar;

Barley and Crab Salad

Servings: **4** • Time: **30** minutes

Ingredients:

- 7 oz barley (already soaked overnight)
- 6 oz crab
- 1 avocado
- 1 lime (juiced)
- ½ onion
- 2 tbsp olive oil
- 1 tsp salt
- Fresh dill to taste

Preparation:

- Steam barley for 20 minutes;
- Steam your crab for 10 minutes, then remove its flesh;
- In the meantime, peel and slice avocado;
- Pour lime juice over avocado slices;
- Peel and slice onion;
- Wash and mince dill;
- In a bowl, mix barley, crab, avocado slices, onion slices and dill;
- Season with olive oil and salt;

Brussels Salad

Servings: **4** • Time: **10 minutes**

Ingredients:

- 3 oz Brussels
- 16 cherry tomatoes
- 1 red onion
- 1 orange (juiced)
- 1 lemon (juiced)
- ½ cup almonds
- 3 tbsp sesame seeds
- 2 tbsp olive oil
- 1 tsp salt
- Fresh thyme to taste

Preparation:

- Wash Brussels and shred them;
- Peel and slice red onion;
- Wash cherry tomatoes and cut them in half;
- Wash, dry and mince thyme;
- In a large bowl, mix shredded Brussels, red onion, cherry tomatoes, almonds, sesame seeds and thyme;
- In a small bowl mix orange juice, lemon juice, olive oil and salt;
- Season your salad with the prepared vinaigrette;

Shrimps and Beans Salad

Servings: **4** • Time: **30** minutes

Ingredients:

- 12 oz shrimps (already cleaned)
- 3 oz beans (already soaked overnight)
- 1 mango
- 1 head lettuce
- 1 orange (juiced)
- 1 cm ginger root
- ½ red onion
- ½ red cabbage
- 2 tbsp olive oil
- 1 tsp salt

Preparation:

- Steam beans for 20 minutes;
- Steam shrimps with ginger for 5 minutes;
- Peel and chop mango and onion;
- Wash and chop lettuce and red cabbage;
- In a large bowl, mix ginger shrimps, mango, red onion, beans, lettuce and red cabbage;
- In a small bowl, mix olive oil, orange juice and salt;
- Season your salad with the prepared vinaigrette

Mango and Scallops Salad

Servings: **4** • Time: **25** minutes

Ingredients:

- 7 oz scallops (already cleaned)
- 2 mangos
- 2 limes
- 1 head lettuce
- ½ head red cabbage
- 1 green pepper
- 1 cucumber
- 1 clove garlic
- 3 tbsp olive oil
- 1 tsp salt
- 1 tsp black pepper
- Fresh mint to taste

Preparation:

- Peel and finely chop garlic;
- Peel and chop mangos;
- Wash, dry and mince mint leaves;
- Put mango in the mixer, together with lime juice, olive oil, garlic, salt, pepper and mint leaves, to obtain a sauce;
- Wash and chop lettuce, red cabbage, green pepper and cucumber;
- Quickly grill your scallops for 2-3 minutes per side;
- In a large bowl, mix scallops, lettuce, red cabbage, green pepper and cucumber;
- Season your salad with the prepared mango sauce;

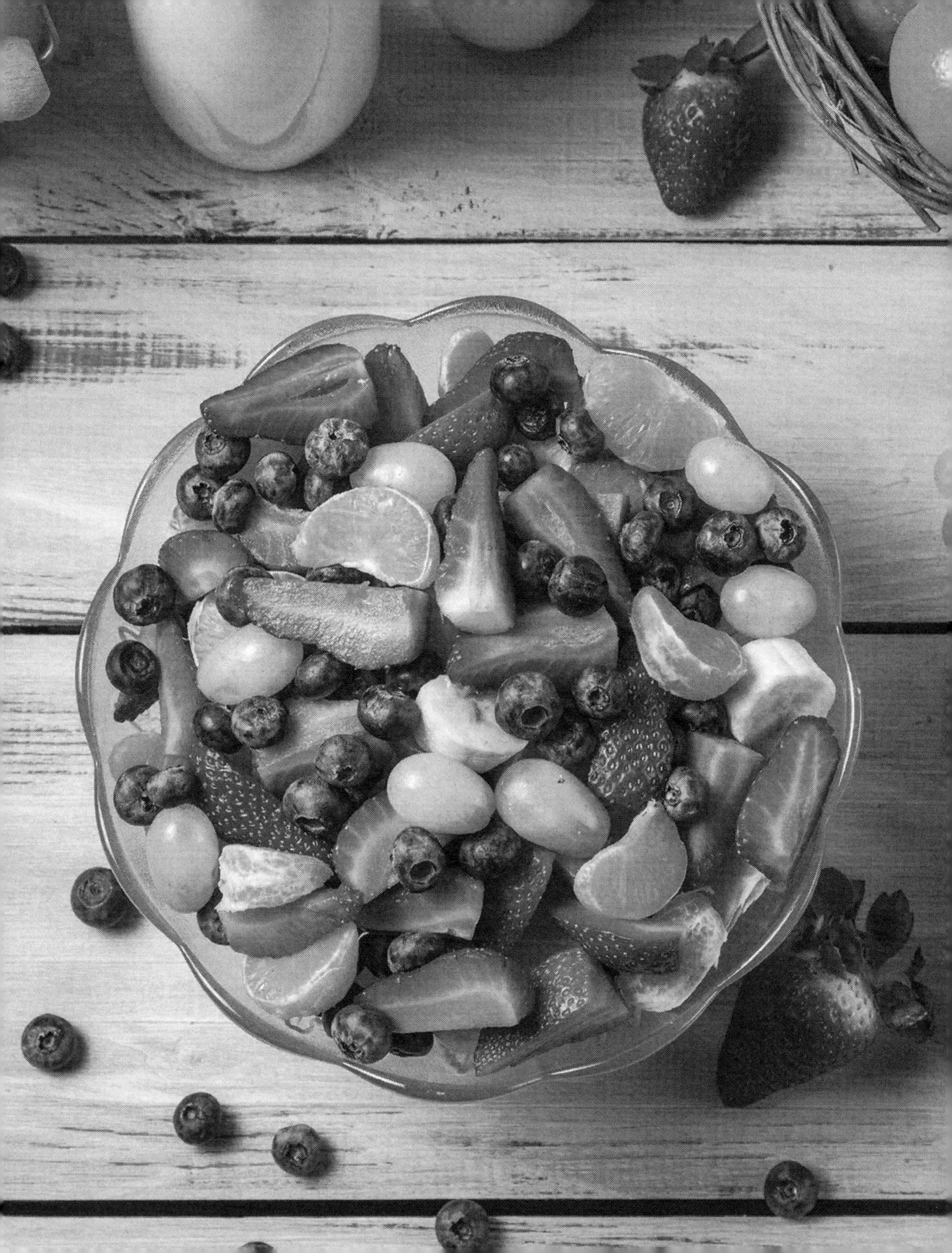

Fresh Tuna and Egg Salad

Servings: **2** • Time: **20** minutes

Ingredients:

- 10 oz fresh tuna
- 2 eggs
- 1 red onion
- 1 stalk celery
- 2 tbsp olive oil
- 2 tsp smoked paprika

Preparation:

- Boil eggs for 10 minutes, then peel them and cut them in half;
- Peel and slice red onion;
- Wash and chop celery;
- Grill your tuna fillet for 2-3 minutes per side, then cut it into small cubes;
- In a bowl, mix tuna, red onion, celery and eggs;
- Season with olive oil and smoked paprika;

Chicken and Melon Salad

Servings: **2** • Time: **20** minutes

Ingredients:

- 8 oz boneless skinless chicken breast
- 2 cups baby spinach
- ½ cup cranberries
- 1 melon
- 1 lemon (juiced)
- 3 tbsp olive oil
- 1 tsp salt
- 1 tsp black pepper
- Fresh basil to taste

Preparation:

- In a small bowl, mix olive oil, lemon juice, salt and pepper;
- Chop your chicken breast and put it into a sterile plastic bag;
- Pour the marinade into the plastic bag and shake it, to let the meat fully absorb the flavors;
- Grill chicken chops for 7-8 minutes per side (depending on their size), while pouring some marinade from time to time to keep them soft and juicy;
- Dice melon;
- Wash and dry baby spinach and basil leaves;
- In a large bowl, mix grilled lemon chicken, melon, baby spinach, cranberries and basil leaves;
- Season with the rest of the marinade;

Edamame Salad

Servings: **4** • Time: **10** minutes

Ingredients:

- 10 oz shelled edamame
- ½ cup sesame seeds
- 2 onions
- 1 sheet nori seaweed
- 2 tbsp apple cider vinegar
- 2 tbsp sesame oil
- 1 tsp salt

Preparation:

- Heat 1 tbsp sesame oil and stir-fry edamame for 5 minutes;
- Roast sesame seeds;
- Peel and slice onions;
- Cut nori seaweed into small stripes;
- In a large bowl, mix edamame, sesame seeds, onions and nori seaweed and season with salt, apple cider vinegar and sesame oil;
- You can accompany your salad with buckwheat savory pancakes;

Barley and Pumpkin Salad

Servings: **2** • Time: **30** minutes

Ingredients:

- 7 oz pumpkin
- 7 oz baby spinach
- 2 oz pomegranate seeds
- 1 cup barley (already soaked overnight)
- 2 tbsp pumpkin seeds
- 2 tbsp olive oil
- 1 tsp salt
- 1 tsp black pepper

Preparation:

- Steam barley for 20 minutes;
- Slice pumpkin and grill it for 5 minutes per side;
- Wash and dry baby spinach;
- In a bowl, mix barley, baby spinach, grilled pumpkin, pomegranate seeds and pumpkin seeds;
- Season with olive oil, salt and pepper;

Quinoa with Beets and Walnuts

Servings: **2** • Time: **25 minutes**

Ingredients:

- ½ cup quinoa
- ½ cup walnuts
- 2 beets
- ½ onion
- 2 tbsp sesame oil
- 1 tsp salt
- 1 tsp black pepper

Preparation:

- Cook quinoa in boiling water for 10 minutes;
- Clean and chop beets;
- Peel and chop onion;
- Heat sesame oil in a non-stick pan and stir-fry beets and onion for 6-7 minutes;
- Adjust with salt and black pepper;
- Serve your quinoa together with stir-fried beets and walnuts;

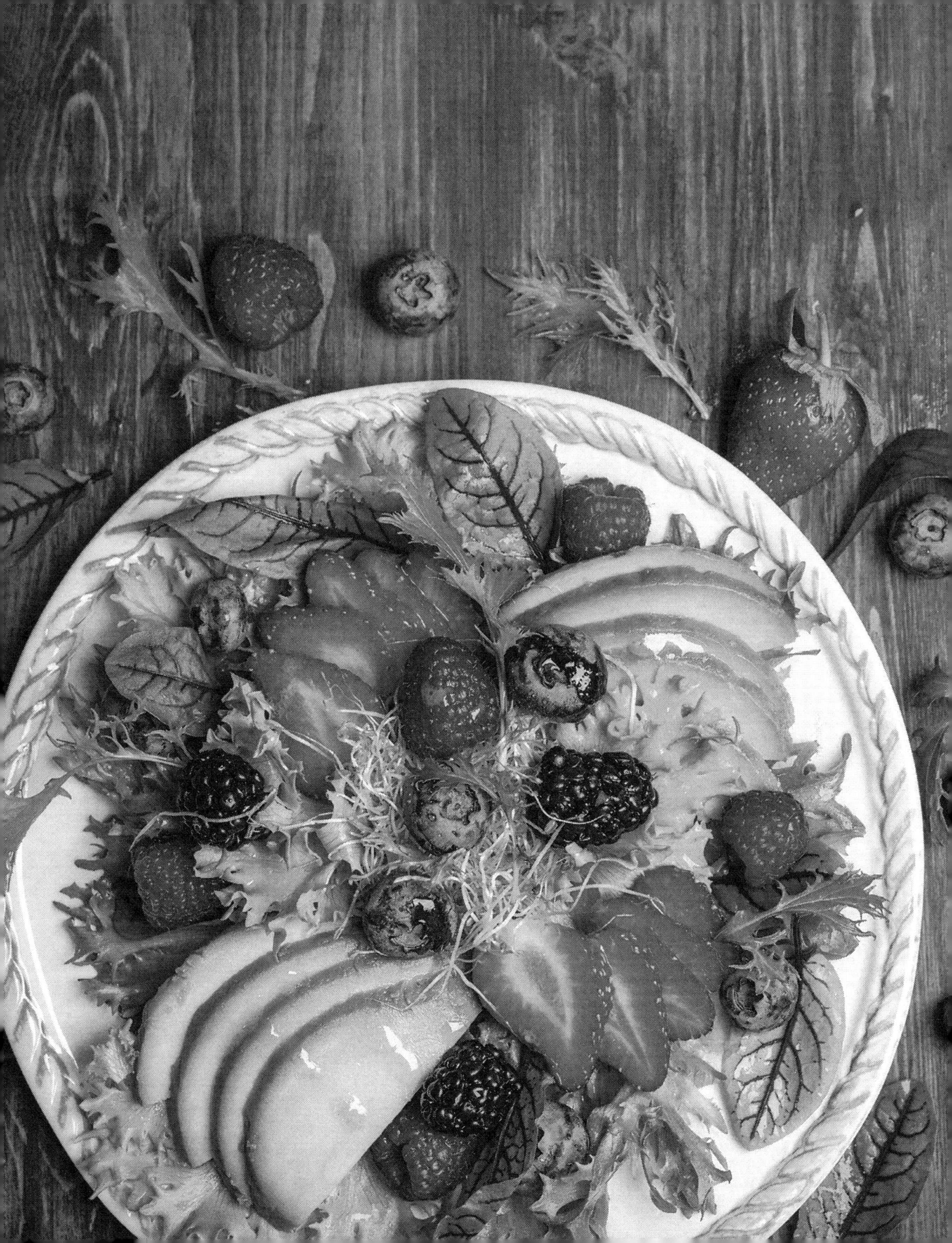

Main Courses

Grilled Lemon Chicken

Servings: **2** • Time: **25** minutes

Ingredients:

- 1 lb boneless skinless chicken breast
- ½ cup olive oil
- ¼ cup lemon juice
- ½ onion
- 1 garlic clove
- 1 tsp black pepper
- 1 tsp salt

Preparation:

- Peel and finely chop your onion;
- In a small bowl, mix olive oil, lemon juice, minced garlic, chopped onion, salt and black pepper to obtain a marinade;
- Chop chicken breast;
- Pour the marinade into a sterile plastic bag and add your chicken chops;
- Shake the bag, to let chicken fully absorb the condiment;
- Grill chicken chops for 7-8 minutes per side (depending on their size), while pouring some marinade from time to time to keep them soft and juicy;
- Serve your grilled chicken with mixed raw vegetables;

Chicken and Asparagus Rolls

Servings: **2** • Time: **30** minutes

Ingredients:

- 12 oz boneless, skinless chicken breast
- 8 asparagus
- 2 spring onions
- 2 tbsp sesame oil
- 1 tsp black pepper
- 1 tsp salt
- Fresh tarragon to taste

Preparation:

- Wash and chop asparagus;
- Peel and finely chop spring onions;
- Wash, dry and mince fresh tarragon;
- Stir-fry chopped asparagus and spring onions in sesame oil for 3-4 minutes, then season with tarragon;
- Slice your chicken breast to obtain 4 thin scallops;
- Rub each scallop with salt and black pepper;
- Place 1 tbsp of cooked vegetables at the center of each scallop and roll it;
- Close each roll with a toothpick;
- Bake at 180°C for 15 minutes;

Grilled Lamb

Servings: **2** • Time: **15 minutes**

Ingredients:

- 1 lb lean lamb chops
- 1 garlic clove
- 1 cm grated ginger root
- 2 tbsp olive oil
- 1 tsp salt
- Fresh rosemary to taste

Preparation:

- Peel and mince garlic;
- Wash, dry and mince rosemary;
- In a small bowl, mix olive oil with minced garlic, grated ginger, minced rosemary and salt;
- Place your lamb chops in a plastic bag and add the marinade;
- Shake your bag to let the meat fully absorb each flavor;
- Grill your lamb chops for 3 minutes per side (according to their size);
- Serve them with a fresh salad or with some grilled vegetables (ex: green peppers);

Garlic Brown Rice with Black Beans

Servings: **2** • Time: **25** minutes

Ingredients:

- 1 cup brown rice
- 1 cup black beans (already soaked overnight)
- 1 cup water
- 2 cloves garlic
- ½ onion
- 1 tbsp olive oil
- 1 tsp coriander seeds
- 1 tsp salt

Preparation:

- Peel and finely chop onion and garlic;
- Place black beans, brown rice, onion, coriander seeds, garlic and olive oil in an instant pot;
- Add also water and salt, stir thoroughly and cook for 20 minutes;

Eggplant Lasagna

Servings: **2** • Time: **30 minutes**

Ingredients:

- 4 tomatoes
- 1 large eggplant
- ½ cup whole-milk cottage cheese
- 1 tbsp olive oil
- 1 tsp salt
- Fresh basil to taste
- Fresh oregano to taste

Preparation:

- Wash and finely slice your eggplant;
- Peel and finely chop tomatoes;
- Wash, dry and mince basil and oregano;
- In a bowl, mix chopped tomatoes with basil, oregano, olive oil and salt;
- Spread some raw tomato sauce over the surface of a baking dish;
- Place some eggplant slices over the tomato sauce;
- Top them with some more tomato sauce;
- Top the sauce with some cottage cheese, then repeat the whole procedure until you have finished all your ingredients;
- Bake at 200°C for 20 minutes;

Turmeric Brown Rice with Edamame

Servings: **2** • Time: **20** minutes

Ingredients:

- 1 cup brown rice
- 1 cup water
- ½ cup shelled edamame
- 1 clove garlic
- 2 tbsp sesame oil
- 2 tsp turmeric
- 1 tsp black pepper
- ½ tsp salt
- Fresh cilantro to taste

Preparation:

- Peel and finely chop garlic;
- Wash, dry and mince cilantro;
- Stir-fry edamame for 5 minutes, together with sesame oil, garlic, salt and pepper;
- Using an immersion blender, mix cooked edamame with a splash of water to obtain a sauce;
- Cook brown rice in an instant pot with turmeric and water for 20 minutes;
- Serve your turmeric brown rice in a bowl topped with garlic-flavored edamame sauce and sprinkle with cilantro leaves;

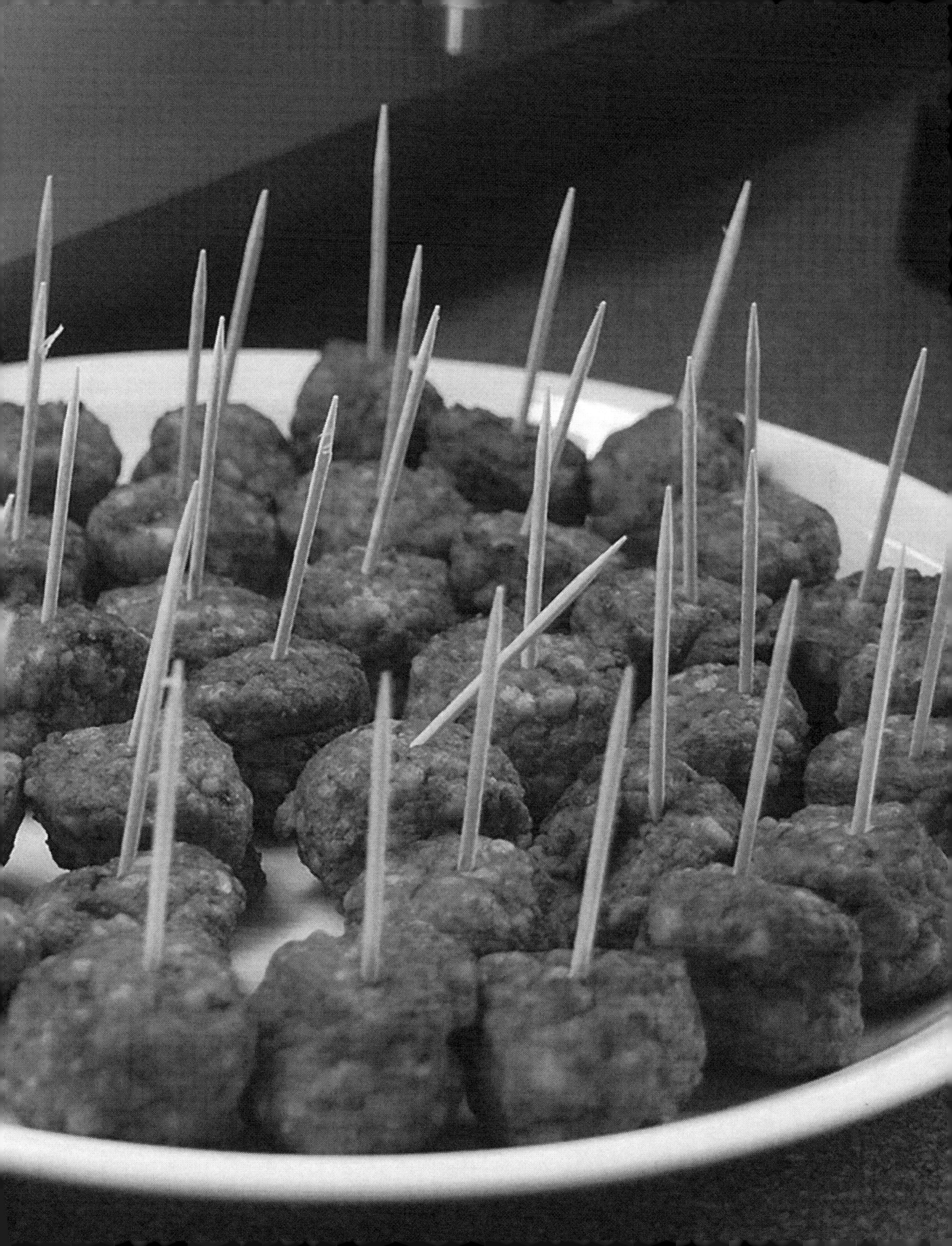

Sesame Salmon

Servings: **4** • Time: **15 minutes**

Ingredients:

- 1 lb salmon
- 3 tbsp sesame oil
- 2 tbsp sesame seeds
- 1 tbsp apple cider vinegar
- 1 tsp salt
- 1 tsp black pepper

Preparation:

- Divide your salmon into 4 smaller fillets;
- Mix sesame seeds with apple cider vinegar, salt and pepper;
- Spread sesame oil over the salmon fillets, then roll them into the sesame seeds mixture;
- Heat 1 tbsp sesame oil in a non-tick pan and cook your fillets for 3-4 minutes per side (paying attention not to burn sesame seeds);
- Serve your sesame salmon with mixed raw vegetables;

Curry Salmon

Servings: **4** • Time: **25** minutes

Ingredients:

- 1 lb 8 oz salmon
- ¾ cup plain yogurt
- ½ lemon (juiced)
- 1 tbsp curry powder

Preparation:

- In a bowl, mix plain yogurt, lemon juice and curry powder to obtain a thick sauce;
- Cut your salmon to obtain 4 smaller fillets;
- Spread 2 tbsp curry sauce over a baking dish;
- Place your salmon fillets onto the baking dish;
- Cover them with the rest of the sauce;
- Bake at 180°C for 20 minutes;
- Serve your curry salmon with roasted vegetables (ex: cherry tomatoes);

Grilled Lamb with Apple Sauce

Servings: **2** • Time: **25 minutes**

Ingredients:

- 6 lean lamb chops
- 2 apples
- 4 tbsp water
- 1 tbsp apple cider vinegar
- 1 tbsp sesame oil
- ½ tsp salt
- ½ tsp black pepper

Preparation:

- Peel and chop your apples;
- Cook them with apple cider vinegar and water for 10 minutes, until soft, then mix with an immersion blender;
- Rub lamb chops with salt, pepper and a few drops of sesame oil;
- Grill lamb chops for 3-4 minutes per side;
- Serve your grilled lamb topped with the warm apple sauce;

Lamb Meatballs

Servings: **4** • Time: **30** minutes

Ingredients:

- 1 lb 8 oz lean lamb
- 2 yolks
- 1 clove garlic
- 1 tsp salt
- 1 tsp black pepper
- Fresh thyme to taste

Preparation:

- Shred lamb meat;
- Peel and finely chop garlic;
- Wash, dry and mince thyme;
- Whisk yolks;
- In a bowl, mix shredded lamb, garlic, thyme, salt, pepper and yolks;
- Shape your meatballs and bake at 200°C for 20 minutes;
- Serve your meatballs with mixed raw vegetables;

Green Tea Halibut

Servings: **4** • Time: **05** minutes

Ingredients:

- 1 lb 8 oz halibut
- 3 cups green tea

Preparation:

- Cut your halibut into cubes;
- Steam your fish for 3-4 minutes, using green tea instead of plain water;
- Serve your halibut with mixed raw vegetables;

Spicy Prawns

Servings: **2** • Time: **15** minutes

Ingredients:

- 7 oz prawns (already cleaned)
- 2 cloves garlic
- 1 tbsp coconut oil
- 2 tsp sweet paprika
- 1 tsp cumin seeds
- 1 tsp black pepper
- ½ tsp salt
- Fresh basil leaves to taste

Preparation:

- Spread some coconut oil over the surface of a baking dish;
- Peel and finely chop garlic;
- Wash and dry basil leaves;
- Place your prawns in the baking dish;
- Sprinkle with paprika, garlic, cumin seeds, salt and pepper;
- Place some basil leaves over the prawns;
- Bake at 200°C for 10 minutes;
- Serve your prawns with some plain brown rice;

Eggs with Beans and Avocado

Servings: **2** • Time: **25** minutes

Ingredients:

- 1 cup black beans (already soaked overnight)
- 4 eggs
- 1 avocado
- 2 tbsp lemon juice
- 1 tbsp olive oil
- ½ tsp salt

Preparation:

- Fill a saucepan with water and bring to the boil;
- Add your eggs and boil for 5 minutes;
- Drain them and delicately peel them;
- Peel and slice avocado;
- Spread lemon juice over avocado slices;
- In the meantime, steam black beans for 20 minutes;
- Place your steamed beans in the mixer with olive oil and salt to obtain a creamy sauce;
- Spread some bean sauce over your plate;
- Top it with avocado slices;
- Place your poached eggs on top of avocado slices;

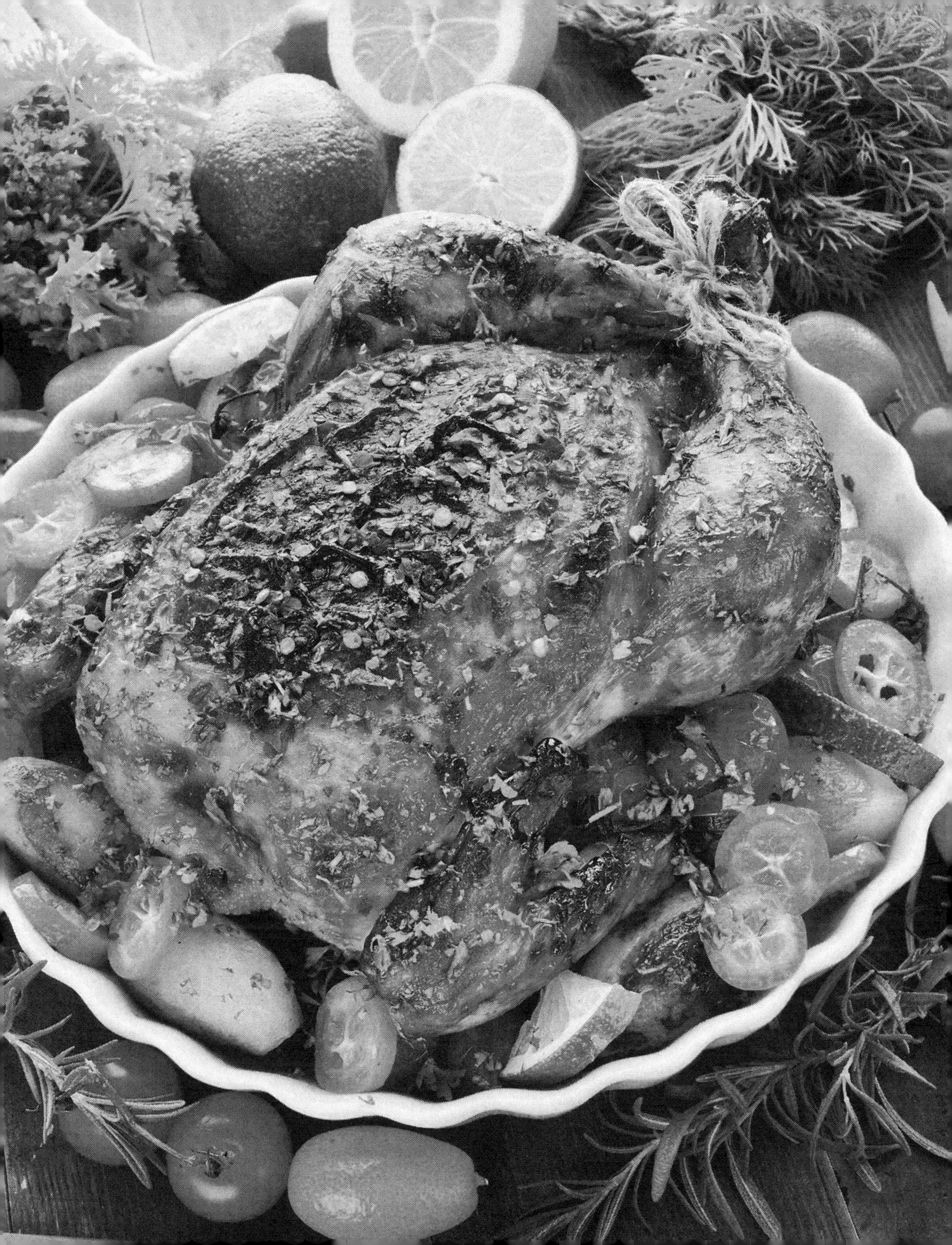

Stir-Fried Veggies

Servings: **4** • Time: **20** minutes

Ingredients:

- 7 oz mushrooms
- 7 oz peas
- 3 carrots
- 2 green peppers
- 1 red onion
- 1 lime (juiced)
- 1 cm grated ginger root
- 3 tbsp coconut oil
- 2 tbsp honey
- 1 tsp black pepper

Preparation:

- Peel and slice red onion;
- Wash and chop green peppers and mushrooms;
- Clean and chop carrots;
- Clean peas;
- Heat coconut oil in a large wok, then add all the vegetables and stir-fry for 6-7 minutes;
- In a small bowl, mix honey with lime juice, black pepper and grated ginger;
- Season your veggies with the prepared sauce;
- You can serve your veggies with grilled tofu;

Instant Pot Garlic Chicken

Servings: **4** • Time: **25** minutes

Ingredients:

- 1 cup water
- 4 chicken tights
- 4 cloves garlic
- ½ onion
- 1 tbsp olive oil
- 1 tsp salt
- 1 tsp black pepper
- Fresh thyme to taste

Preparation:

- Peel and chop garlic cloves and onion;
- Wash, dry and mince thyme;
- Pour water into your instant pot;
- Add salt, black pepper, garlic cloves, onion and thyme;
- Add also your chicken tights;
- Add also olive oil and stir, to make sure all the flavors will mix;
- Cook for 20 minutes;
- You can serve your garlic chicken with baked potatoes;

Chickpea Burger

Servings: **2** • Time: **30** minutes

Ingredients:

- 1 cup chickpeas (already soaked overnight)
- 1 onion
- 1 egg
- 1 tsp salt

Preparation:

- Steam chickpeas for 20 minutes;
- Peel and finely chop the onion;
- Put steamed chickpeas in the mixer with egg, onion and salt to obtain a creamy texture;
- Shape your burgers;
- Grill them for a couple of minutes per side;
- You can serve them with homemade guacamole sauce and some lettuce;

Broccoli Burger

Servings: **2** • Time: **30** minutes

Ingredients:

- 1 cup broccoli florets
- ½ cup grated parmesan cheese
- 2 oz cous cous
- 2 shallots
- 1 egg
- 2 tsp cumin seeds

Preparation:

- Steam broccoli for 15 minutes;
- Cook cous cous in boiling water for 5 minutes;
- Peel and finely chop shallots;
- Place your steamed broccoli in the mixer, together with cumin seeds, egg and chopped shallots;
- Place the mixture in a bowl and add parmesan cheese and cous cous;
- Stir thoroughly;
- Shape your burgers;
- Grill them for a couple of minutes per side;
- You can serve them with a plain yogurt and dill dip and some mixed raw vegetables;

Veggie Balls

Servings: **4** • Time: **30** minutes

Ingredients:

- 1 cup lentils (already soaked overnight)
- ¼ cup grated parmesan cheese
- 2 egg yolks
- 2 carrots
- 1 onion
- 1 celery stalk
- 1 tbsp olive oil
- 1 tsp salt
- Fresh thyme to taste

Preparation:

- Peel and finely chop, onion and carrots;
- Clean and finely chop celery;
- Wash, dry and mince thyme;
- Steam your vegetables for 15 minutes, then place them in the mixer with olive oil, egg yolks, parmesan cheese, salt and thyme;
- Shape your balls and bake them at 200°C for 10 minutes;
- Serve them with a homemade dip and some lettuce;

Fish Balls

Servings: **4** • Time: **30** minutes

Ingredients:

- 5 oz fresh tuna
- 2 egg yolks
- 1 red onion
- 1 potato
- 1 tsp salt
- Fresh parsley to taste

Preparation:

- Peel and chop your potato;
- Peel and finely chop onion;
- Wash, dry and mince parsley;
- Steam your potato for 15 minutes;
- Steam also chopped tuna for 5 minutes;
- Place tuna, potato, egg yolks, chopped onion, parsley and salt in the mixer, to obtain a homogeneous mixture;
- Shape your balls;
- Bake them at 180°C for 10 minutes;
- Serve them with a homemade dip and some lettuce;

Grilled Chicken with Peppers

Servings: **2** • Time: **25** minutes

Ingredients:

- 1 lb boneless, skinless chicken breast
- 2 green peppers
- 1 yellow pepper
- 1 red pepper
- 1 red onion
- 2 tbsp olive oil
- 1 tsp salt
- 1 tsp black pepper

Preparation:

- Peel and finely chop red onion;
- Wash all the peppers and cut them in half (removing their seeds);
- Place chopped green pepper and red onion in the mixer, together with olive oil, salt and black pepper to obtain a thick sauce;
- Chop your chicken breast and put it into a sterile plastic bag;
- Pour the sauce in the plastic bag and shake it, to let the meat fully absorb the flavors;
- Grill chicken chops for 7-8 minutes per side (depending on their size);
- In the meantime, grill also your colored peppers;
- Serve your grilled chicken and peppers topped with the remaining sauce;

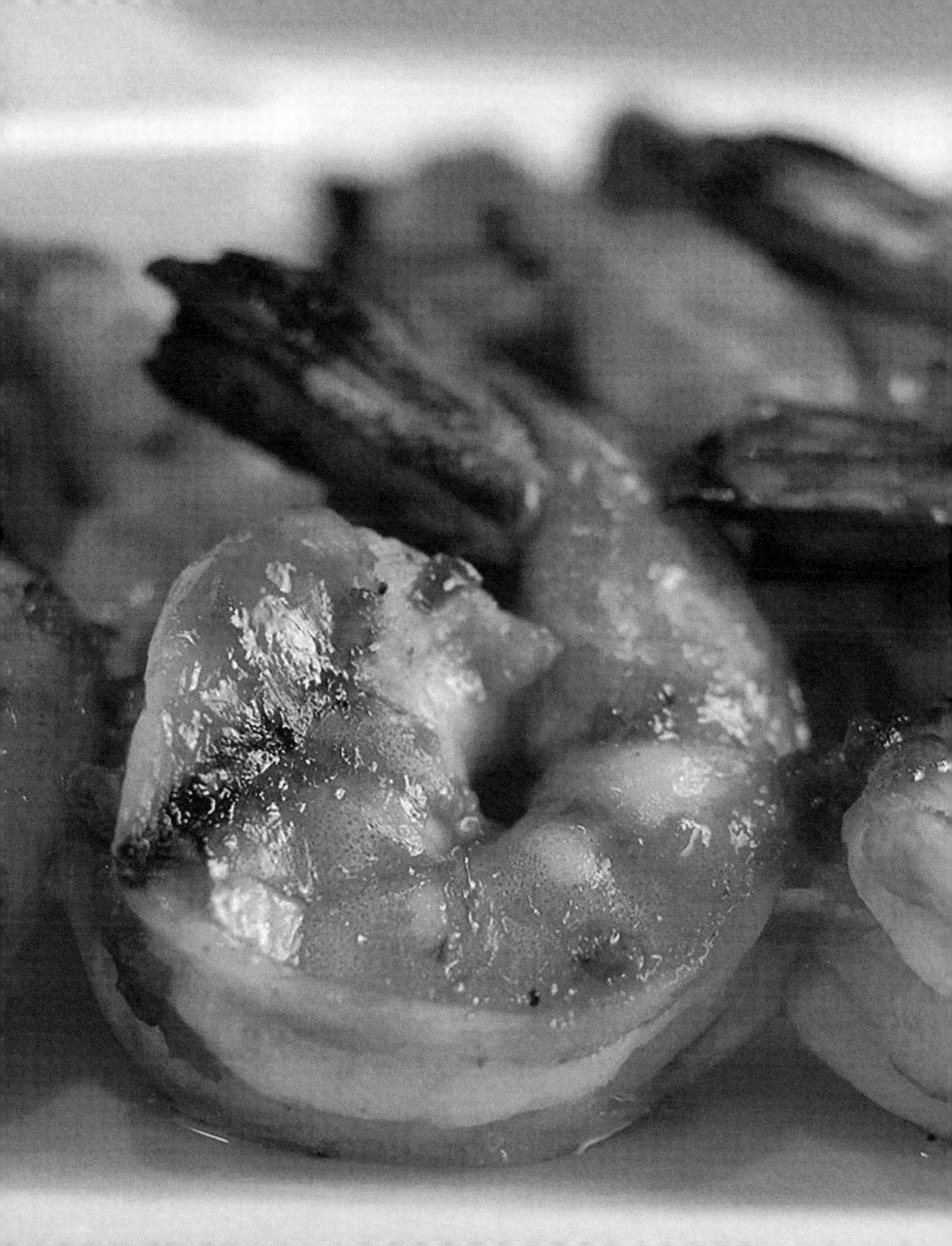

Pumpkin and Chicken Curry

Servings: **2** • Time: **30** minutes

Ingredients:

- 10 oz boneless, skinless chicken breast
- 7 oz pumpkin
- 1 cup coconut milk
- 2 tomatoes
- ½ onion
- 1 clove garlic
- 1 cm grated ginger root
- 2 tbsp sesame oil
- 2 tsp curry powder
- 1 tsp mustard seeds

Preparation:

- Peel and finely chop onion and garlic;
- Grate raw pumpkin;
- Peel and finely chop tomatoes;
- Cut chicken breast into small stripes;
- Heat mustard seeds in a non-stick pan, until they release their aroma, then add sesame oil, onion, garlic and ginger;
- Stir fry grated pumpkin and chicken stripes for 7-8 minutes;
- Add coconut milk, a splash of water, chopped tomatoes and curry powder and cook over medium heat for 10 minutes;
- Serve it together with some plain brown rice;

Eggplant Burger

Servings: **4** • Time: **25** minutes

Ingredients:

- 2 eggplants
- 1 clove garlic
- 3 tbsp grated parmesan cheese
- 2 tbsp sesame oil
- 1 tsp salt
- 1 tsp black pepper
- Fresh tarragon to taste

Preparation:

- Wash your eggplants and finely chop them;
- Peel and finely chop garlic;
- Wash, dry and mince fresh tarragon;
- Heat some sesame oil in a non-stick pan and stir-fry eggplants for 5 minutes;
- Place your eggplants in a bowl together with grated parmesan cheese, garlic, salt, pepper and tarragon;
- Stir thoroughly to obtain a homogeneous mixture;
- Shape your burgers;
- Bake them at 200°C for 10 minutes;
- You can serve them together with some mixed raw vegetables;

Walnut Burger

Servings: **4** • Time: **30** minutes

Ingredients:

- ½ cup brown rice
- ½ cup walnut
- 1 carrot
- 1 egg
- ½ onion
- 1 tbsp sesame oil
- 2 tsp salt
- 1 tsp black pepper

Preparation:

- Cook brown rice in an instant pot for 15 minutes;
- In the meantime, peel and finely chop onion and carrot;
- Stir-fry onion and carrot with sesame oil for 5 minutes;
- Chop walnuts;
- In a bowl, mix brown rice, onion, carrot, walnuts, egg, salt and black pepper;
- Shape your burgers;
- Bake them at 200°C for 10 minutes;
- You can serve them with grilled vegetables (ex: grilled onions)

Brown Rice with Beans

Servings: **2** • Time: **25** minutes

Ingredients:

- 1 cup black beans (already soaked overnight)
- 1 cup brown rice
- ½ cup diced pumpkin
- 1 clove garlic
- ½ onion
- 1 tsp salt
- 1 tsp black pepper
- Fresh rosemary to taste

Preparation:

- Peel and finely chop onion and garlic;
- Wash and dry rosemary;
- Steam black beans and chopped pumpkin for 20 minutes;
- In the meantime, place your brown rice in an instant pot with water, onion, garlic and rosemary;
- Cook rice for 20 minutes;
- In a bowl, mix brown rice, black beans and pumpkin and with salt and black pepper;

Cauliflower and Chickpea Curry

Servings: **4** • Time: **30** minutes

Ingredients:

- 1 lb cauliflower
- 12 oz chickpeas (already soaked overnight)
- 1 cup coconut milk
- 1 onion
- 1 clove garlic
- 2 tbsp coconut oil
- 2 tsp curry powder
- 1 tsp cumin seeds
- 1 tsp turmeric

Preparation:

- Peel and finely chop onion and garlic;
- Steam chickpeas for 10 minutes;
- Wash and cut cauliflower into florets;
- Heat coconut oil in a non-stick pan and add onion, garlic, turmeric, curry powder and cumin seeds;
- Add cauliflower and chickpeas;
- Add also coconut milk and a splash of water and cook over medium heat for 15 minutes;
- You can serve it with plain brown rice;

Brown Rice with Beets

Servings: **2** • Time: **25** minutes

Ingredients:

- 1 cup brown rice
- 2 beets
- 2 cloves garlic
- 1 tbsp sesame oil
- 1 tsp salt
- Fresh basil to taste

Preparation:

- Cook brown rice in an instant pot for 20 minutes;
- In the meantime, peel and dice beets, then steam them for 20 minutes;
- Peel and finely chop garlic;
- Wash and dry basil leaves;
- Place your beets in the mixer with garlic, sesame oil and salt;
- Serve your brown rice topped with the beet sauce and some fresh basil leaves;

Quinoa with Eggplants

Servings: **2** • Time: **25 minutes**

Ingredients:

- 1 cup quinoa
- ¾ cup almonds
- 1 large eggplant
- 2 tbsp olive oil
- 2 tbsp apple cider vinegar
- 2 tsp sweet paprika
- Fresh oregano to taste

Preparation:

- Cook quinoa in boiling water and sweet paprika for 20 minutes;
- Wash and chop your eggplant and steam it for 15 minutes;
- Roast almonds;
- Wash, dry and mince oregano,
- In a bowl, mix spicy quinoa, steamed eggplant and roasted almonds;
- Season with olive oil, apple cider vinegar and sprinkle with minced oregano;

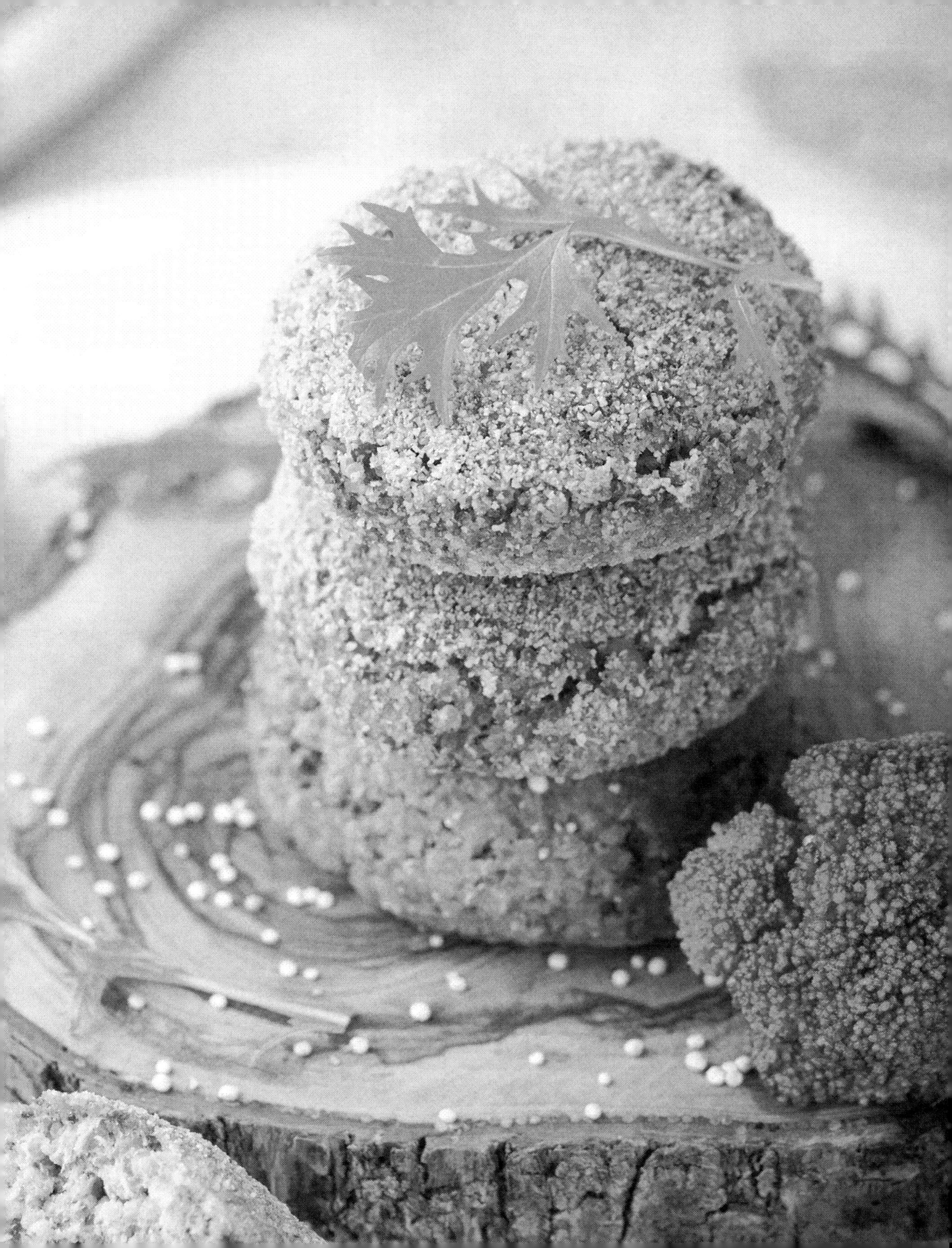

Spicy Edamame with Shrimps

Servings: **4** • Time: **20** minutes

Ingredients:

- 1 lb shrimps (already cleaned)
- 1 cup shelled edamame
- 1 lemon (juiced)
- 1 clove garlic
- 2 tbsp sesame oil
- 1 tsp mustard seeds
- 1 tsp black pepper
- 1 tsp cumin seeds
- Fresh cilantro leaves to taste

Preparation:

- Peel and finely chop garlic;
- Wash and dry cilantro leaves;
- Stir-fry edamame for 5 minutes, together with sesame oil, garlic, black pepper, mustard seeds and cumin seeds;
- Pour lemon juice over shrimps and bake them at 180°C for 10 minutes;
- Sprinkle your shrimps with cilantro leaves and serve them together with spicy edamame;

Cous Cous with Stir-Fried Veggies

Servings: **2** • Time: **25 minutes**

Ingredients:

- 1 cup cous cous
- 2 zucchinis
- 2 carrots
- 1 sweet potato
- 1 turnip
- 3 tbsp sesame oil
- 1 tsp black pepper
- 1 tsp turmeric
- 1 tsp cumin seeds
- 1 tsp nutmeg
- Fresh cilantro leaves to taste

Preparation:

- Peel and chop sweet potato, turnip, zucchinis and carrots;
- Wash and dry cilantro leaves;
- Cook cous cous in boiling water for 10 minutes;
- In a large pan, heat 2 tbsp sesame oil with black pepper, turmeric, cumin seed and nutmeg;
- Add chopped vegetables and stir-fry for 7-8 minutes;
- In a bowl, mix cous cous with stir-fried veggies, then season with some more sesame oil and sprinkle with cilantro leaves;

Salmon Fillet with Ginger Apple Sauce

Servings: **4** • Time: **25** minutes

Ingredients:

- 1 lb salmon
- 3 apples
- 1 lemon (juiced)
- 1 cm grated ginger root

Preparation:

- Peel and chop your apples;
- Place them in a pan with lemon juice and ginger root and cook them for 10 minutes;
- Mix with an immersion blender to obtain a sauce;
- Cut your salmon to obtain 4 smaller fillets;
- Steam salmon fillets for 15 minutes;
- Serve your steamed salmon fillets topped with the ginger apple sauce;
- You can serve them with steamed vegetables (ex: steamed broccoli);

Orange Chicken

Servings: **4** • Time: **15** minutes

Ingredients:

- 1 lb boneless skinless chicken breast
- 4 oranges (juiced)
- 1 cm grated ginger root
- 2 tbsp sesame oil
- 1 tsp black pepper

Preparation:

- Slice your chicken breast;
- In a non-stick pan, heat sesame oil and quickly cook chicken (thin scallops will cook faster);
- Pour orange juice in the pan;
- Add also grated ginger and black pepper and turn your chicken scallops to make them fully absorb the condiment;
- You can serve your orange chicken topped with the remaining cooking sauce and accompany them with steamed vegetables (ex: steamed broccoli);

Basil Grilled Vegetables

Servings: **4** • Time: **15 minutes**

Ingredients:

- ½ cup basil leaves
- 4 zucchinis
- 4 tomatoes
- 2 onions
- 2 cloves garlic
- 1 lemon (juiced)
- 1 eggplant
- 2 tbsp sesame oil
- 1 tsp cumin seeds

Preparation:

- Wash, dry and slice all the vegetables;
- Was, dry and mince basil leaves;
- Peel and chop garlic;
- Place lemon juice, sesame oil, garlic, cumin seeds and basil leaves in the mixer to obtain a sauce;
- Grill your vegetables for 3 minutes per side and serve them topped with the basil sauce;
- You can accompany them with some steamed fish;

Steamed Chicken with Brussels

Servings: **4** • Time: **30** minutes

Ingredients:

- 1lb boneless skinless chicken breast
- 3 cups Brussels
- 1 clove garlic
- 1 cm grated ginger root
- 2 tbsp olive oil
- 1 tsp salt

Preparation:

- Cut your chicken breast into small cubes;
- Peel and mince garlic;
- Wash Brussels and cut them in half;
- In a small bowl, mix olive oil, garlic, salt and ginger to obtain a marinade;
- Place your chicken chops into a sterile plastic bag;
- Pour the marinade into the plastic bag and shake it to let the meat fully absorb the flavors;
- Steam your marinated chicken for 10 minutes;
- Add also Brussels and the rest of the marinade and continue steaming for another 10 minutes;

Barley with Mushrooms

Servings: **4** • Time: **25** minutes

Ingredients:

- 1 cup barley (already soaked overnight)
- 2 oz shiitake mushrooms
- 1 clove garlic
- 1 bay leaf
- ½ onion
- 1 tbsp sesame oil
- 1 tsp salt
- 1 tsp black pepper
- Grated parmesan cheese to taste

Preparation:

- Wash and slice shiitake mushrooms;
- Peel and slice onion;
- Peel and chop garlic;
- Heat some sesame oil in a non-stick pan and stir-fry mushrooms, onion and garlic for 5 minutes;
- Steam barley for 20 minutes, together with a bay leaf;
- Add it to the pan with mushrooms;
- Cook for another 3-4 minutes;
- Adjust with salt and black pepper and serve your barley sprinkled with grated parmesan cheese;

Eggs and Veggies

Servings: **4** • Time: **25** minutes

Ingredients:

- 4 eggs
- 2 turnips
- 1 sweet potato
- 1 red onion
- 1 green pepper
- 2 tbsp sesame oil
- 1 tsp salt
- Fresh parsley to taste

Preparation:

- Peel and chop sweet potato, turnips and onion;
- Wash and chop green pepper;
- Wash, dry and mince parsley;
- Steam your vegetables for 15 minutes;
- Heat sesame oil in a large pan and add ¼ of your vegetables;
- Adjust with salt;
- Break 1 egg on top of your vegetables and let it harden;
- Repeat the procedure until you have finished all your ingredients;
- Serve your eggs sprinkled with minced parsley;

Veggie Skewers

Servings: **4** • Time: **15 minutes**

Ingredients:

- 5 oz tofu
- ½ cup broccoli florets
- ½ cup mushrooms
- 8 cherry tomatoes
- 2 zucchinis
- 1 yellow pepper
- 2 tbsp lemon juice
- 2 tbsp sesame oil
- 1 tsp salt
- 1 tsp black pepper

Preparation:

- Wash and chop pepper and zucchinis and mushrooms;
- Wash broccoli and cherry tomatoes;
- Chop tofu;
- In a small bowl, mix sesame oil, lemon juice, salt and black pepper;
- Pour the condiment over vegetables and tofu and toss them, to make sure they fully absorb it;
- Compose your skewers and grill them for 2-3 minutes per side

Hazelnut Chicken

Servings: **4** • Time: **20** minutes

Ingredients:

- 1 lb boneless skinless chicken breast
- ½ cup hazelnuts
- 1 clove garlic
- 2 tbsp sesame oil
- 1 tsp salt
- 1 tsp black pepper

Preparation:

- Roast your hazelnuts, then chop them;
- Peel and chop garlic:
- Shred chicken breast;
- Heat sesame oil in a non-stick pan with garlic and stir-fry shredded chicken for 3-4 minutes;
- Add also roasted hazelnuts, salt and black pepper and cook for another 3-4 minutes;
- You can serve your hazelnut chicken with stir-fried veggies (ex: green beans);

Lamb with Red Onion Sauce

Servings: **4** • Time: **30 minutes**

Ingredients:

- 1 lb 8 oz lamb chops
- 7 oz cous cous
- 3 red onions
- 3 tbsp sesame oil
- 1 tbsp saffron powder
- 1 tsp salt
- 1 tsp black pepper
- Fresh oregano to taste

Preparation:

- Peel and finely chop red onions;
- Wash and mince oregano leaves;
- Heat 2 tbsp sesame oil in a non-stick pan and stir-fry onions for 6-7 minutes;
- Place them in the mixer with some more sesame oil, salt and black pepper, to obtain a thick sauce;
- Steam lamb chops with saffron and oregano for 20 minutes;
- In the meantime, cook cous cous in boiling water for 10 minutes;
- Serve your lamb chops topped with red onion sauce and accompany them with cous cous;

Grilled Bass with Spring Onions

Servings: **2** • Time: **15** minutes

Ingredients:

- 6 spring onions
- 2 sea bass fillets
- 1 lemon (juiced)
- 2 cm grated ginger root
- 4 tbsp olive oil

Preparation:

- Rub your fillets with olive oil and grated ginger and grill them for about 5 minutes per side (depending on the size);
- In the meantime, steam spring onions for 10 minutes;
- Serve your grilled fish together with spring onions and season with lemon juice;

Spicy Cauliflower

Servings: **4** • Time: **30 minutes**

Ingredients:

- 1 cauliflower
- 2 tbsp olive oil
- 2 tsp cumin seeds
- 2 tsp black pepper
- 1 tsp turmeric
- 1 tsp coriander seeds

Preparation:

- Wash and cut your cauliflower into florets;
- In a small bowl, mix olive oil, cumin seeds, coriander seeds, black pepper and turmeric;
- Rub the florets with the seasoning;
- Bake them at 200° for 20 minutes;
- You can serve your spicy cauliflower together with steamed chicken breast;

Chicken Chili

Servings: **4** • Time: **30** minutes

Ingredients:

- 1 lb boneless skinless chicken breast
- 10 oz black beans (already soaked overnight)
- 5 tomatoes
- 2 cloves garlic
- 1 onion
- 2 tbsp olive oil
- 2 tsp cumin seeds
- 2 tsp chili flakes
- 1 tsp black pepper

Preparation:

- Shred your chicken breast;
- Steam black beans for 20 minutes;
- Steam chicken for 5 minutes;
- In the meantime, peel and finely chop tomatoes, onion and garlic;
- In a large pan, heat olive oil and add onion, garlic, cumin seeds, chili flakes and black pepper;
- Add also chopped tomatoes and cook for 6-7 minutes;
- Add also black beans and chicken and cover with water;
- Cook for 10 minutes;

Mediterranean Chicken

Servings: **4** • Time: **20** minutes

Ingredients:

- 1 lb boneless skinless chicken breast
- 5 tomatoes
- 2 garlic cloves
- 1 onion
- 2 tbsp olive oil
- 1 tsp salt
- 1 tsp black pepper
- Fresh oregano to taste

Preparation:

- Peel and finely chop tomatoes, onion and garlic;
- Wash, dry and mince oregano;
- Heat olive oil in a large pan and add tomatoes, onion and garlic;
- Cook for 10 minutes, until you obtain a thick sauce;
- Adjust with salt and pepper;
- In the meantime, slice your chicken breast to obtain 4 scallops;
- Grill chicken for 3-4 minutes per side;
- Serve your grilled chicken topped with tomato sauce and sprinkled with oregano;
- You can serve it together with mixed raw vegetables;

Lime Salmon

Servings: **2** • Time: **15** minutes

Ingredients:

- 12 oz salmon
- 2 limes (juiced)
- 1 cm grated ginger root
- 2 tbsp olive oil
- 1 tbsp honey
- 1 tsp black pepper

Preparation:

- Cut your salmon to obtain 2 smaller fillets;
- In a small bowl, mix lime juice, honey, ginger, olive oil and black pepper;
- Spread the marinade over your salmon fillets;
- Grill them for 5 minutes per side (depending on their size);
- You can serve it together with some plain brown rice and some fresh lettuce;

Snacks/Appetizers

Sweet Potato Waffles

Servings: **4** • Time: **30** minutes

Ingredients:

- 3 eggs
- 2 large sweet potatoes
- 1 tbsp coconut oil
- 2 tsp sweet paprika
- 1 tsp salt

For the topping:

- Avocado
- Baby spinach

Preparation:

- Peel sweet potatoes and grate them;
- In a bowl, mix grated sweet potatoes with whisked eggs;
- Add paprika and salt and stir thoroughly;
- Spread coconut oil over the waffle maker;
- Add ¼ of the mixture and cook until it becomes crunchy;
- Repeat the procedure until you have used all your mixture;
- Serve your waffles topped with baby spinach and sliced avocado

Pepper Omelet

Servings: **2** • Time: **20** minutes

Ingredients:

- 2 whole eggs
- 2 egg whites
- ½ green pepper
- ½ yellow pepper
- ½ onion
- 2 tbsp sesame oil
- ½ tsp salt

Preparation:

- Wash and chop peppers;
- Peel and finely chop onion;
- Heat sesame oil in a large pan and stir-fry peppers and onion for 5 minutes;
- In the meantime, whisk eggs in a small bowl and adjust with salt;
- Pour whisked eggs into the pan and cook for another 4-5 minutes,
- Turn the omelet and cook for another 3 minutes;
- Serve hot, together with mixed raw vegetables;

Vegetarian Wraps

Servings: **2** • Time: **20** minutes

Ingredients:

- 3 oz soft goat cheese
- 2 carrots
- 2 cucumbers
- ½ head of lettuce
- 1 tbsp coconut oil
- 2 tsp coriander seeds
- ½ tsp black pepper

Preparation:

- Peel and grate carrots and cucumbers;
- In a bowl, mix grated carrots and cucumber with coconut oil, coriander seeds, black pepper and goat cheese;
- Wash and dry lettuce leaves;
- Place 2 tbsp of your veggie and cheese mixture in the middle of each leave and roll it;
- You can prepare your wraps in the morning and leave them in the fridge all day, to let all the flavors mix together;

Buckwheat Pancakes with Broccoli and Leek

Servings: **4** • Time: **25** minutes

Ingredients:

- 4 oz broccoli
- 2 oz buckwheat flour
- ½ cup water
- 1 leek
- 1 egg
- 2 tbsp coconut oil
- 1 tsp salt
- 1 tsp black pepper
- Flaxseeds to taste
- Grated parmesan cheese to taste

Preparation:

- In a bowl, mix buckwheat flour, flaxseeds, salt and pepper;
- Add whisked egg and stir;
- Pour also water and 1 tbsp coconut oil into the bowl and stir thoroughly;
- Pour 1 tbsp coconut oil into a non-stick pan and add ¼ of the mixture;
- Cook 2-3 minutes per side;
- Repeat the procedure until you have finished all your mixture;
- Clean and chop broccoli and leek, then steam them for 5 minutes;
- Season them with grated parmesan cheese;
- Place some vegetables on one side of a pancake and fold it over;
- Repeat the procedure for every pancake;

Zucchini Pancakes with Leek and Avocado

Servings: **4** • Time: **30 minutes**

Ingredients:

- ½ cup oat flour
- 6 egg whites
- 2 zucchinis
- 1 leek
- 1 avocado
- ½ onion
- ½ lemon (juiced)
- 2 tbsp sesame oil
- ½ tsp salt
- ½ tsp black pepper
- Fresh cilantro leaves to taste

Preparation:

- Peel and grate zucchinis;
- Peel and finely chop the onion;
- In a bowl, mix zucchini, onion, egg whites, oat flour, salt and pepper;
- Spread 1 tbsp sesame oil over the surface of a non-stick pan and add ¼ of the mixture;
- Cook 2-3 minutes per side;
- Repeat the procedure until you have finished all your mixture;
- Clean and slice leek and avocado;
- Wash and dry cilantro leaves;
- Season leek and avocado slices with lemon juice, sesame oil and fresh cilantro leaves;
- Serve your zucchini pancakes topped with raw leek and avocado;

Scrambled Eggs with Mushrooms

Servings: **2** • Time: **25** minutes

Ingredients:

- 6 mushrooms
- 4 egg whites
- 2 whole eggs
- 1 clove garlic
- ¾ onion
- 1 tbsp olive oil
- 1 tsp salt
- Whole wheat bread to taste

Preparation:

- Carefully wash your mushrooms and slice them;
- Whisk eggs in a bowl;
- Peel and finely chop onion and garlic and add them to the whisked eggs;
- Adjust with salt and stir thoroughly;
- Heat olive oil in a non-stick pan and add sliced mushrooms;
- Cook over medium heat for 10 minutes;
- Add the egg mixture to the pan and cook for 5 minutes, while stirring to make scrambled eggs;
- Serve your scrambled eggs together with whole wheat bread;

Turmeric Quinoa Balls

Servings: **4** • Time: **30** minutes

Ingredients:

- 1 cup quinoa
- 2 yolks
- 1 clove garlic
- ½ onion
- 1 tbsp flaxseeds
- 2 tsp turmeric
- ½ tsp salt
- Fresh basil to taste

Preparation:

- Carefully rinse quinoa and cook it in boiling water for 15 minutes;
- In the meantime, peel and finely chop onion and garlic, then wash and mince basil leaves;
- In a bowl, mix cooked quinoa, flaxseeds, onion, garlic, basil leaves, turmeric and salt;
- Add also the egg yolks and stir thoroughly;
- Shape your balls and bake them at 180°C for 10 minutes;
- Serve your quinoa balls with mixed raw vegetables;

Lentil Falafel

Servings: **4** • Time: **30** minutes

Ingredients:

- 1 cup lentils (already soaked overnight)
- 2 cloves garlic
- 1 carrot
- ½ onion
- 2 tbsp whole wheat flour
- 1 tbsp lemon juice
- 1 tsp cumin seeds
- 1 tsp smoked paprika
- ½ tsp nutmeg powder
- ½ tsp black pepper
- Fresh parsley to taste
- Fresh oregano to taste

Preparation:

- Peel and finely chop carrot, onion and garlic;
- Wash, dry and mince parsley and oregano;
- Mix softened lentils with garlic, carrot, onion, lemon juice, parsley, oregano, cumin, paprika, nutmeg, pepper and a splash of water;
- Add whole wheat flour and shape your falafel;
- Bake at 200°C for 20 minutes;
- You can serve your lentil falafel with a plain yogurt and dill dip;

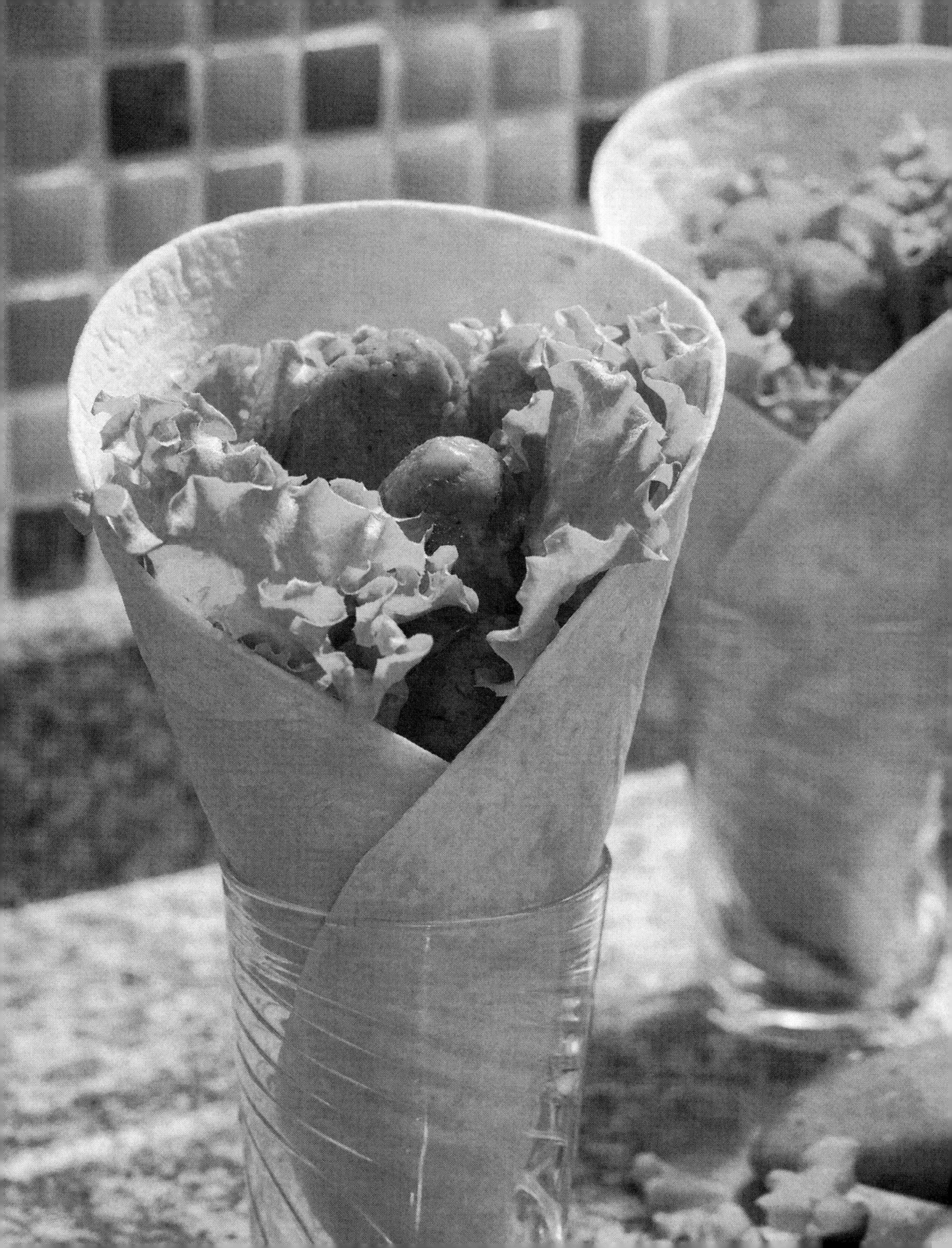

Savory Oatmeal

Servings: **4** • Time: **25 minutes**

Ingredients:

- 9 oz asparagus
- 3 shallots
- 3 cups water
- 1 cup oatmeal (already soaked overnight)
- 2 tbsp sesame oil
- 1 tsp salt
- 1 tsp black pepper
- Fresh mint leaves to taste

Preparation:

- Boil oatmeal in hot water for 5 minutes;
- Peel and slice shallots;
- Clean and chop asparagus;
- Wash, dry and mince mint leaves;
- Heat sesame oil in a non-stick pan and quickly cook asparagus and shallots (7-8 minutes);
- Drain oatmeal and add it to the pan;
- Adjust with salt and pepper and stir for another 2-3 minutes;
- Serve your savory oatmeal sprinkled with mint leaves;

Hummus with veggies

Servings: **4** • Time: **25** minutes

Ingredients:

- 7 oz chickpeas (already soaked overnight)
- 1 clove garlic
- ½ lemon (juiced)
- 1 tbsp olive oil
- 1 tbsp sunflower seeds butter
- 1 tsp cumin seeds
- 1 tsp salt
- Fresh parsley to taste
- Celery to taste
- Carrots to taste
- Cherry tomatoes to taste
- Radishes to taste
- Whole wheat bread to taste

Preparation:

- Steam chickpeas for 20 minutes, then put them in the mixer with lemon juice to obtain a creamy texture;
- Add salt, sunflower seeds butter, cumin seeds, olive oil and chopped garlic and mix again;
- Sprinkle your hummus sauce with minced fresh parsley;
- Wash and chop celery, carrots, cherry tomatoes and radishes;
- Serve your hummus as a dip for raw vegetables and bread;

Sweet Potato Muffins

Servings: **about 10 muffins** • Time: **30** minutes

Ingredients:

- 1 ½ cup whole wheat flour
- ½ cup plain yogurt
- ½ cup grated parmesan cheese
- 1 large sweet potato
- 1 egg
- 1 tsp baking powder
- 1 tsp salt

Preparation:

- Peel and chop your sweet potato;
- Steam it for 10 minutes;
- Put it in the mixer, together with egg, salt, yogurt and parmesan cheese;
- Add also whole wheat flour and baking powder;
- Stir thoroughly to obtain a homogeneous batter;
- Fill your muffin tins and bake at 180°C for 15 minutes;
- You can serve your muffins with mixed raw vegetables;

Cottage Cheese Savory Pancakes

Servings: **4** • Time: **25** minutes

Ingredients:

- 1 cup cottage cheese
- 1/2 cup whole wheat flour
- 8 egg whites
- 1 potato
- 1 tbsp sesame oil
- 1 tsp baking powder
- 1 tsp salt

Preparation:

- Peel, slice and steam your potato for 15 minutes;
- Put your steamed potato in the mixer, together with cottage cheese and egg whites;
- Add whole wheat flour, salt and baking powder to the mixture and stir thoroughly to obtain a homogeneous batter;
- Spread 1 tbsp sesame oil over the surface of a non-stick pan and add ¼ of the mixture;
- Cook 2-3 minutes per side;
- Repeat the procedure until you have finished all your mixture;
- You can top your savory pancakes with some sliced tomatoes and some fresh arugula;

Salmon Rolls with Avocado Sauce

Servings: **4** • Time: **15** minutes

Ingredients:

- 6 oz salmon
- 2 avocados
- 1 yellow pepper
- 1 lime (juiced)
- Fresh cilantro leaves to taste

Preparation:

- Peel and grate avocados;
- Wash, dry and mince cilantro leaves;
- In a bowl, mix grated avocadoes with cilantro leaves and lime juice and stir until you obtain a creamy texture;
- Wash your yellow pepper and cut it into small stripes;
- Finely slice your salmon fillet to obtain several thin layers;
- Place one slice of salmon over a flat surface and top it with 1 tbsp avocado sauce;
- Place 2 pepper stripes at the center of the salmon slice and roll it;
- Repeat the procedure until you have finished all your ingredients:
- You can serve salmon rolls with some mixed raw vegetables;

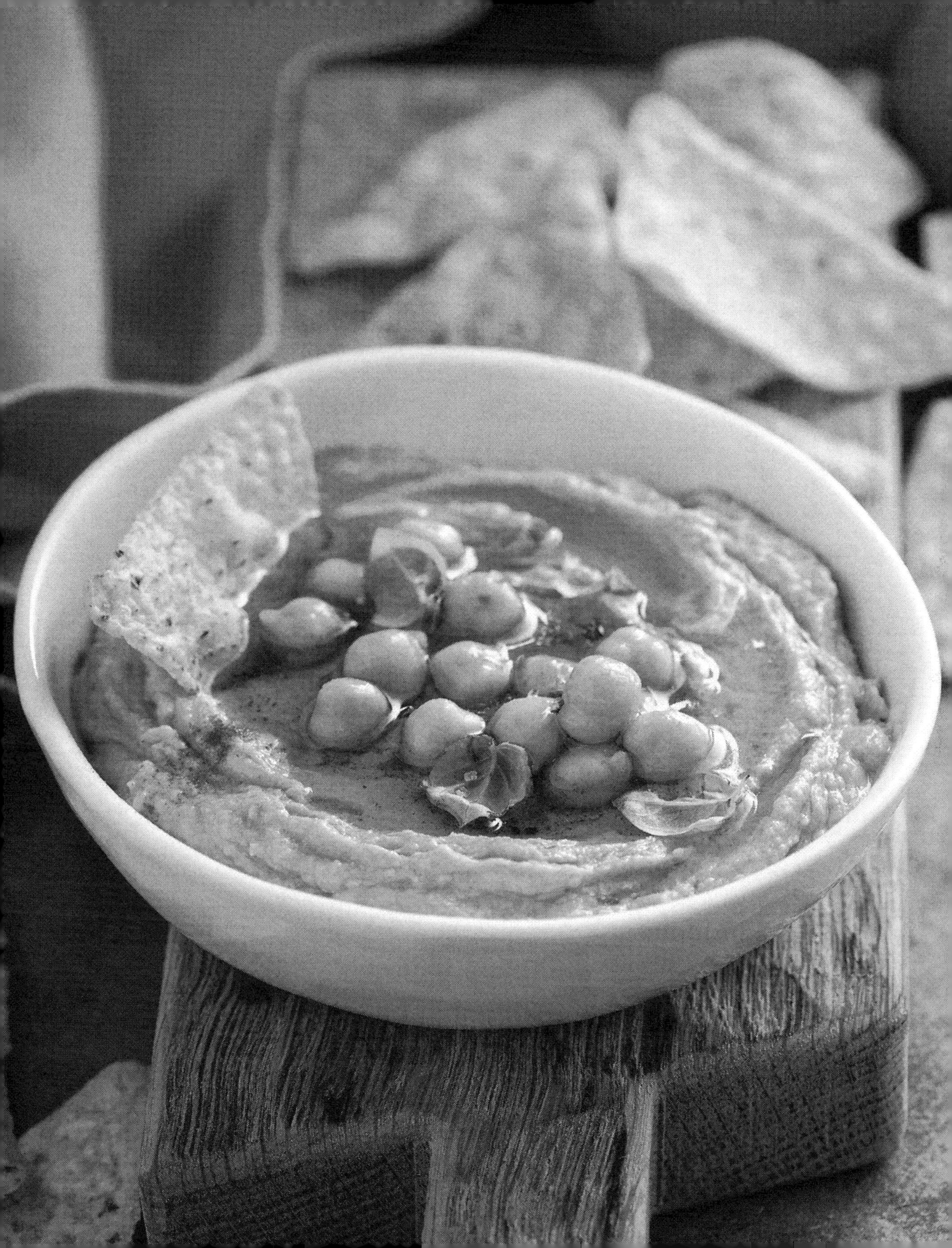

Soups

Leek and Potato Soup

Servings: **2** • Time: **30** minutes

Ingredients:

- 4 oz potatoes
- 3 cups water
- 1 leek
- 1 stalk celery
- 1 carrot
- ½ onion
- 1 tbsp olive oil
- 1 tsp salt
- 1 tsp black pepper
- Sesame seeds to taste

Preparation:

- Peel and chop potatoes and onion;
- Clean and chop celery and leek;
- Heat olive oil in a large pan and add chopped vegetables;
- Add also water and cook over high heat for 20 minutes;
- Mix with an immersion blender to obtain a creamy texture;
- Adjust with salt and pepper;
- Serve sprinkled with sesame seeds to taste;

Shrimp Soup

Servings: **2** • Time: **30** minutes

Ingredients:

- 12 oz fresh shrimps
- 2 tomatoes
- 1 shallot
- ½ green pepper
- 1 clove garlic
- 1 cup coconut milk
- 1 cup water
- 2 tbsp sesame oil
- 1 tsp salt

Preparation:

- Peel and finely chop shallot and tomatoes;
- Wash and finely chop your green pepper;
- Peel and mince garlic;
- Stir-fry shallot, green pepper and tomatoes in sesame oil for 3-4 minutes and adjust with salt;
- Add water, minced garlic and coconut milk;
- Stir thoroughly and cook over low heat for 20 minutes;
- In the meantime, clean and steam your shrimps for 2 minutes;
- Add shrimps to the soup only 2-3 minutes before the end of the cooking;

Carrot and Coconut Soup

Servings: **2** • Time: **30** minutes

Ingredients:

- 2 cups coconut milk
- 4 carrots
- 1 onion
- 1 clove garlic
- 1 cm grated ginger root
- 2 tbsp coconut oil
- 1 tsp cumin seeds
- Fresh cilantro leaves to taste

Preparation:

- Peel and slice onion;
- Peel and mince garlic;
- Peel and chop carrots;
- Wash, dry and mince cilantro leaves;
- Stir fry onion and carrots with coconut oil for 6-7 minutes;
- Pour 1 cup water in the pan and bring to the boil;
- Add coconut milk, minced garlic, grated ginger and cumin seeds and mix with an immersion blender to obtain a creamy soup;
- Cook for another couple of minutes and serve sprinkled with cilantro leaves;

Spinach and Broccoli Soup

Servings: **4** • Time: **30** minutes

Ingredients:

- 4 cups broccoli florets
- 4 cups spinach
- 2 tbsp olive oil
- 1 tsp salt
- 1 tsp black pepper
- Fresh oregano to taste

Preparation:

- Wash, dry and mince oregano;
- Wash broccoli and spinach and place them in a large pan filled with water;
- Add also salt and pepper and bring to the boil;
- Cook over high heat for 15 minutes;
- Mix with an immersion blender;
- Serve with a few drops of raw olive oil and sprinkle with oregano;

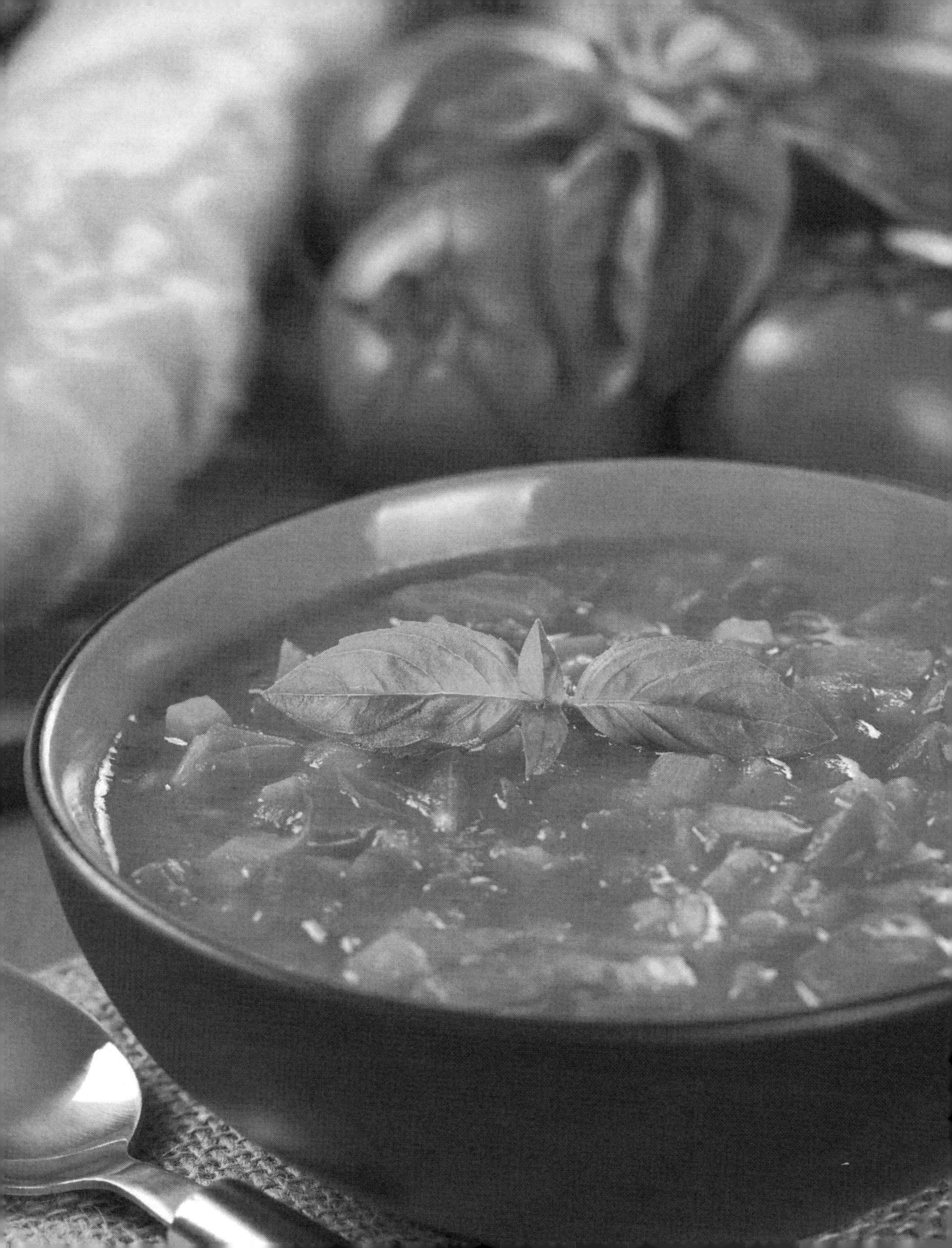

Ginger Bean Cream

Servings: **4** • Time: **30 minutes**

Ingredients:

- 12 oz white beans (already soaked overnight)
- 2 bay leaves
- 1 onion
- 1 carrot
- 1 clove garlic
- 2 cm grated fresh ginger root
- 2 tbsp sesame oil
- 1 tsp black pepper

Preparation:

- Steam your beans with bay leaves for 20 minutes;
- Peel and finely chop onion, garlic and carrot;
- Heat sesame oil in a large pan and add onion, garlic, carrot, ginger and black pepper;
- Stir-fry for 5 minutes;
- Cover with water and add steamed beans, then cook for another 10 minutes;
- Mix with an immersion blender to obtain a cream;

Tomato Soup

Servings: **4** • Time: **30** minutes

Ingredients:

- 8 tomatoes
- 2 carrots
- 1 onion
- 1 tbsp olive oil
- 2 tsp salt
- 1 tsp black pepper
- Fresh rosemary to taste

Preparation:

- Peel, slice and steam carrots and onion for 10 minutes;
- Roast tomatoes in the oven at 180° for 15 minutes;
- Remove their peel and place their pulp in a large pan;
- Add olive oil, onion, carrots, salt and pepper and cover with water;
- Cook over high heat for 10 minutes, then mix with an immersion blender to obtain a creamy texture;
- Serve your soup sprinkled with fresh rosemary;

Cauliflower Soup

Servings: **4** • Time: **30** minutes

Ingredients:

- 2 cups of cauliflower florets
- 1 potato
- 1 onion
- 1 clove garlic
- 1 tbsp coconut oil
- 2 tsp sweet paprika
- Fresh dill to taste

Preparation:

- Peel and chop potato, onion and garlic;
- Wash, dry and mince dill;
- Heat coconut oil and sweet paprika in a large pan and stir-fry potato, onion, cauliflower and garlic for 5 minutes;
- Cover with water and cook over high heat for 20 minutes, then mix with an immersion blender to obtain a creamy texture;
- Serve your soup topped with minced dill;

Carrot and Ginger Soup

Servings: **4** • Time: **25** minutes

Ingredients:

- 1 cup water
- ½ cup green tea
- 5 carrots
- ½ leek
- ½ stalk celery
- 1 cm grated ginger root
- 1 tbsp sesame oil
- 1 tsp salt
- 1 tsp coriander seeds

Preparation:

- Clean and chop leek, celery and carrots;
- Heat sesame oil in a large pan and stir-fry leek, celery and carrots with grated ginger and coriander seeds;
- Add green tea, water and salt and cook for 15 minutes;
- Mix with an immersion blender to obtain a creamy texture;

Mushroom Soup

Servings: **4** • Time: **30** minutes

Ingredients:

- 4 oz mushrooms
- 2 carrots
- 1 stalk celery
- ½ onion
- 1 clove garlic
- 2 tbsp olive oil
- 1 tsp salt
- 1 tsp black pepper
- Fresh thyme to taste
- Fresh parsley to taste

Preparation:

- Peel and finely chop onion, garlic and carrots;
- Wash and slice mushrooms;
- Wash and finely chop celery;
- Wash, dry and mince thyme and parsley;
- Heat olive oil in a large pan and add chopped vegetables;
- Add salt, pepper and cook for about 10 minutes;
- Cover with water and bring to the boil;
- Cook for another 10 minutes and mix with an immersion blender, to obtain a creamy texture;
- Serve your soup sprinkled with parsley and thyme;

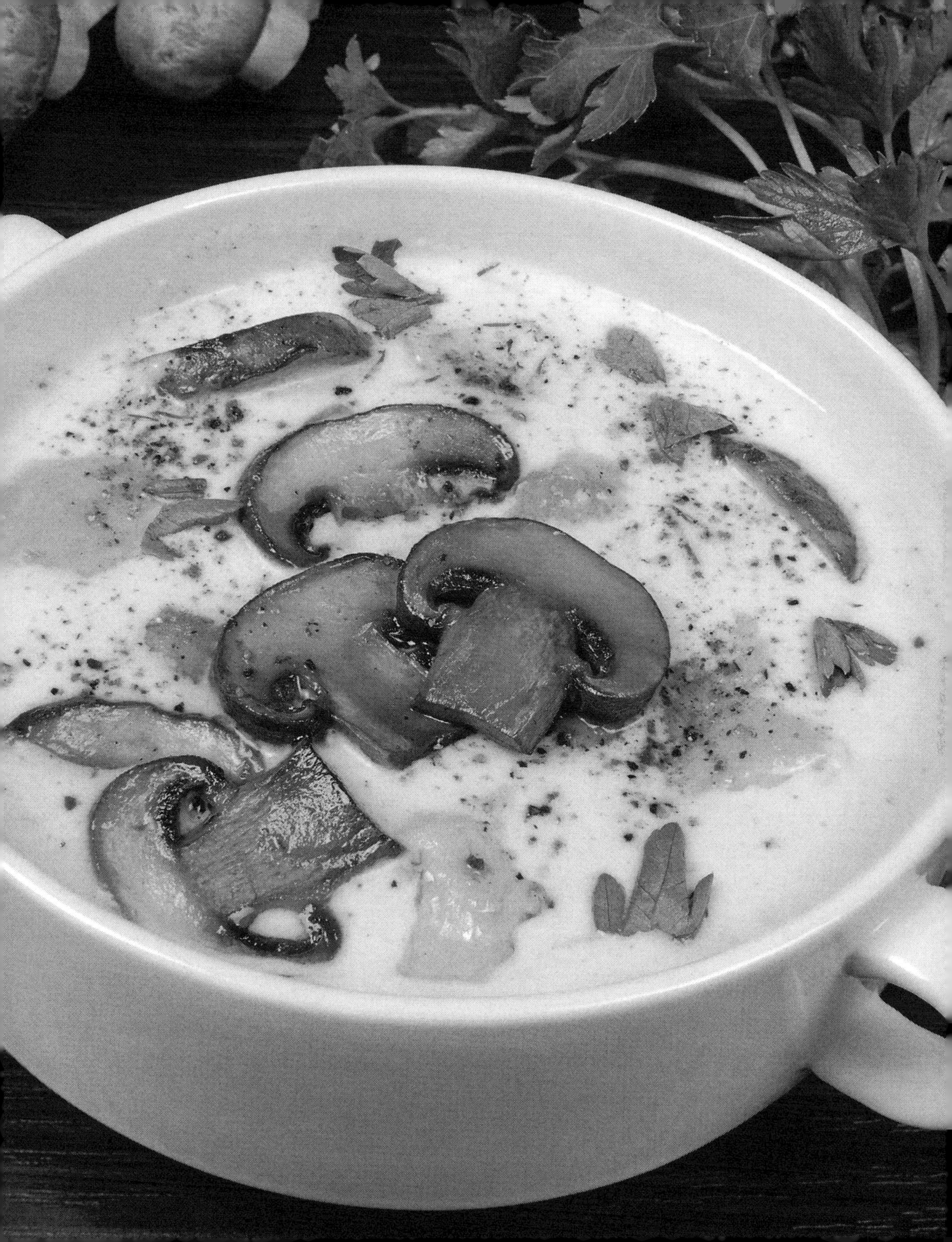

Claim Your Free Bonus

Weekly meal plan & Grocery Shopping List

Our goal is not just to inspire you with healthy recipes but also encourage you to try them inside your kitchen as a step towards adopting a healthier lifestyle. Therefore, to make things super easy for you, our team has created a 7-day meal plan and a grocery shopping list to accompany it.

Go to www.tamarindpress.com/clean-eating-bonus to download the handy PDF.

If you enjoyed reading the book, don't forget to leave a quick review inside Amazon. As a token of thanks, we'll send you the ebook version of our next cookbook (absolutely for FREE!). Just drop us an email to review@tamarindpress.com after you review the book to claim another awesome cookbook!

Conversion Chart

AMERICAN/ENGLISH MEASUREMENTS	METRIC MEASUREMENTS
½ oz	10 gr
¾ oz	20 gr
1 oz	25 gr
1 ½ oz	40 gr
2 oz	50 gr
2 ½ oz	60 gr
3 oz	75 gr
4 oz	110 gr
4 ½ oz	125 gr
5 oz	150 gr
6 oz	175 gr
7 oz	200 gr
8 oz	225 gr
9 oz	250 gr
10 oz	275 gr
12 oz	350 gr
1 lb	450 gr
1 lb 8 oz	700 gr
2 lb	900 gr
1 cup liquid	240 ml
½ cup liquid	120 ml
¼ cup liquid	60 ml
1 tbsp liquid	15 ml
1 tsp liquid	5 ml
1 cup flour	150 gr
1 cup sugar	175 gr
1 cup rice	180 gr